Talal Hamad Aladwani

Carriage of Goods by Sea:

The Obligation of the Charterers' to Direct the Vessel to Safe Ports

VDM Verlag Dr. Müller

Impressum/Imprint (nur für Deutschland/ only for Germany)

Bibliografische Information der Deutschen Nationalbibliothek: Die Deutsche Nationalbibliothek verzeichnet diese Publikation in der Deutschen Nationalbibliografie; detaillierte bibliografische Daten sind im Internet über http://dnb.d-nb.de abrufbar.

Alle in diesem Buch genannten Marken und Produktnamen unterliegen warenzeichen-, marken- oder patentrechtlichem Schutz bzw. sind Warenzeichen oder eingetragene Warenzeichen der jeweiligen Inhaber. Die Wiedergabe von Marken, Produktnamen, Gebrauchsnamen, Handelsnamen, Warenbezeichnungen u.s.w. in diesem Werk berechtigt auch ohne besondere Kennzeichnung nicht zu der Annahme, dass solche Namen im Sinne der Warenzeichen- und Markenschutzgesetzgebung als frei zu betrachten wären und daher von jedermann benutzt werden dürften.

Coverbild: www.ingimage.com

Verlag: VDM Verlag Dr. Müller GmbH & Co. KG
Dudweiler Landstr. 99, 66123 Saarbrücken, Deutschland
Telefon +49 681 9100-698, Telefax +49 681 9100-988
Email: info@vdm-verlag.de
Zugl.: university of swansea, diss., 2008

Herstellung in Deutschland:
Schaltungsdienst Lange o.H.G., Berlin
Books on Demand GmbH, Norderstedt
Reha GmbH, Saarbrücken
Amazon Distribution GmbH, Leipzig
ISBN: 978-3-639-32489-1

Imprint (only for USA, GB)

Bibliographic information published by the Deutsche Nationalbibliothek: The Deutsche Nationalbibliothek lists this publication in the Deutsche Nationalbibliografie; detailed bibliographic data are available in the Internet at http://dnb.d-nb.de.

Any brand names and product names mentioned in this book are subject to trademark, brand or patent protection and are trademarks or registered trademarks of their respective holders. The use of brand names, product names, common names, trade names, product descriptions etc. even without a particular marking in this works is in no way to be construed to mean that such names may be regarded as unrestricted in respect of trademark and brand protection legislation and could thus be used by anyone.

Cover image: www.ingimage.com

Publisher: VDM Verlag Dr. Müller GmbH & Co. KG
Dudweiler Landstr. 99, 66123 Saarbrücken, Germany
Phone +49 681 9100-698, Fax +49 681 9100-988
Email: info@vdm-publishing.com

Printed in the U.S.A.
Printed in the U.K. by (see last page)
ISBN: 978-3-639-32489-1

Talal Aladwani

Carriage of Goods by Sea

The Charterers' Obligation to Direct the vessel to Safe Ports

i

Abstract

In most charterparties, a clause such as Ěbetween safe ports and safe placesŠ is to be found and this imposes a primary obligation on the charterers to order the ship only to ports which, at the time when their order was given, are prospectively safe. The purpose of this book is to give a picture of the rights and obligations in regard to such clauses. It will also discuss the clause of implied obligation.

Following an introduction to the subject in chapter 1, a definition extracted from *The Eastern City* regarding the safe port term is given in Chapter 2 with a critical analysis to the elements of the safe port definition.

The significant differences between the implied and express warranty of safety obligation is discussed in Chapter 3. Here the differences are explained by giving some examples of types of implied warranties encapsulating with case law. The scope of obligation between different provisions in some charterparties for the purpose of lowering the level of obligation is also examined.

Chapter 4 is concerned with the rights and obligations between the shipowners and the charterers in terms of renominating a safe port, the time of the duty to rise and the right to consider or reject the order. In this chapter, the effect of the negligent on the part of the master is considered. Apportionment of liability between the owner and the charterer is also considered in light of the contributory negligence act.

Chapter 5 is devoted to the potential legal ramifications on the implementation of the International Codes (ISM, ISPS) and regulations (Risk Assessment) in shipŇ master decision making to proceed to a safe port, and how such ramifications may influence the judicial decisions.

A general conclusion of the book is given in chapter 6

This study is based on the case law, information and materials available to me on 28th Oct. 2008.

Talal Aladwani

Plymouth University

January 2011

Acknowledgment

My thanks are due and gladly offered to my beloved parents, Borthers; Hiatham, Bassam and Ali. Many thanks to my friends who stood beside me and encouraged me all the time especially Qais Albesher, Mohammad Almutairi and all who help me throughout this study.

Finally, I would like to thank my sponsors KOTC/KPC leaded by Shiakha Shatha Alsubah. Thank you to all of them for believing in me.

Contents Page

Abstract ii

Acknowledgements iii

List of Cases vii

Abbreviations x

Chapter One 'Introduction'... 1

Chapter Two 'What Constitutes a Safe Port?'.................... 8

    2.1 What is a safe port?..9

    2.2 First: the ÈRelevant period of timeŠ................................. 10

        2.2.1Temporary dangers..13

        2.2.2 Delay...14

    2.3 Second: ÈThe particular shipŠ...15

    2.4 Third: ÈReach it, use it and return from itŠ.......................16

        2.4.1 Local warnings..17

        2.4.2 Port set-up Infrastructure and mooring facilities...................18

        2.4.3 Navigational aids...19

2.4.4 Political unsafety..19

2.5 Fourth: ÈAbnormal eventsŠ..20

2.6 Fifth: ÈDangerous which cannot/can be avoided by good navigation and seamanshipŠ...22

Chapter Three: What is the difference between express and implied warranty of safety obligation? 26

3.1 Express warranty 27

3.2 When does the implied warranty to be implied? 28

3.3 Alternative wording or provision to lower level of scope of obligation 32

3.3.1 ÈDue DiligenceŠ 32

3.3.2 ÈSo near thereto as she may safely getŠ 35

3.3.3 ÈWar clauseŠ 37

3.3.4 ÈEmployment and indemnity provisionsŠ 38

Chapter Four: Rights and obligations of charterers/shipowners - the difference between voyage and time charterers obligation in terms of port renomination?...40

4.1 What is the difference between voyage and time charterers' obligation in terms of port renomination?..41

4.2 When does the time chartererŠ duty to renominate a safe port arise?..43

4.3 Under the ownerŠ right to consider or reject the order, should the vessel proceed into an unsafe port?...45

4.4 Negligence on the part of the master or navigation.....................47

4.5 Contributory negligence...50

Chapter Five: Potential legal ramifications on the implementation of the International Codes (ISM, ISPS) and regulations (Risk Assessment) in ship's master decision making to proceed to a safe port, and how such ramifications may influence the judicial.......................................52

5.1 How useful are the International Codes (ISM, ISPS) and regulations (risk assessment) to the master in determining whether a port is a safe port?.....53

5.2 First: How can the ISM code to be used by the tribunal in order to evaluate the liability?..53

5.3 Second: How can the ISPS code be used judicially to uncover the shipowner̃ negligence?..54

5.4 Risk assessment...56

5.4.1 Risk assessment into practice...58

5.4.2 How does the risk assessment̃ flow chart work according to each phase?..58

Chapter Six: Conclusion..62

Glossary 67

Bibliography 69

List of Cases

AB Marintrans v. *Comet Shipping Co. Ltd* [1985] 1 W.L.R. 1270

Aegean Sea Traders Corp v. *Repsol Petroleo SA (The Aegean Sea)* [1998] 2 Lloyd's Rep. 39, p.68

Aktieselskabet Wriksen v. *Foy, Morgan & Co.* (1926) 25 Ll.L.R. 442

Alhambra [1881] LR 6 PD 68

Archimidis (2007) 2 Ll Rep 101

Athamas (Owners) v. *Dig Vigay Cement Co. (The Athamas)* [1963] 1 Lloyd$\tilde{\text{N}}$ Rep.287 (C.A.)

Atkins International v. *Islamic Republic of Iran Shipping Lines (The APJ Priti)* [1987] 2 Lloyd$\tilde{\text{N}}$ Rep. 37

Bastifell v. ___**Llyd**___ (1862) 1 H. & C. 388

Brostrom, A. & Son v. *Dreyfus, L. & Co.* (1932) 44 Ll. L. Rep.136 (1932) 38 Com. Cas. 79

Bulk Shipping v. *Ipco Trading S.A. (The Jasmine B)* [1992] 1 Lloyd$\tilde{\text{N}}$ Rep. 39

Compania Naviera Maropan S/A v. *Bowater's Lloyd Pulp and Paper Mills Limited (The Stork)* [1955] 2 QB 68

Dahl v. *Velson* (1880) 6 App. Cas.38

De Meza v. *Apple* [1974] 1 Lloyd$\tilde{\text{N}}$ Rep. 508

Dow-Europe v. *Novokla Inc.* [1998] 1 Lloyd$\tilde{\text{N}}$ Rep 306

Duncan v. *Koster (The Teutonia)* (1872) L.R. 4 P.C. 17

Emeh v. *Kensington & Chelsea & Westminster Area Health Authority* [1985] Q.B. 1012

Evans v. *Bullock* (1877) 38 LT 34

Fornyade Rederiaktiebolaget Commercial v. *Blake & Co. (The Varing)* (1931) 39 Ll. L. Rep. 205 [1931] p.79, at p.87

Generally Reardon Smith Line Ltd. v. *Australian Wheat Board (The Houston City)* [1954] 2 Lloyd$\tilde{\text{N}}$ Rep. 148

Goodbody v. *Balfour Williamson* [1899] 5 Com. Cas. 59 [1932] 44 Ll L Rep 136, p. 137

GW Grace & Co Ltd v. *General Steam Navigation Co. Ltd* (The Sussex Oak) [1950] 2 KB 383

Hall v. *Paul* [1914] 19 Com. Cas. 384 M

Horsley v. *Price* (1883) 11 Q.B.D. 244

Johnson v. *Saxon Queen Steamship (The Saxon Queen)* (1913) 108 L.T. 564

Kawasaki Kisen Kabushiki of Kobe v. *Bantham S.S. Co, Ltd* [1939] 2 K.B. 544

Knutsford S.S. Ltd. v. *Tillmans & Co.* [1908] A.C. 406

Kodros Shipping Corp of Monrovia v. *Empresa Cubana de Fletes (The Evia* (No.2)) [1981] 2

Lloyd's Rep. 613; [1982] 1 Lloyd's Rep. 334 (CA); [1983] 1 A.C. 736 (HL)

Kristiandsands *Tankeri* v. *Standard (Bahamas) (The Polyglory)* [1977] 2 LloydÑ Rep.353

Kuwait Petroleum Corp v. *I & D Oil Carriers Ltd (The Houda)* [1994] 2 LloydÑ Rep. 541

Larrinaga v. *The King* (1944) 78 LL. Rep 167

Leeds Shipping Co. v. *Societe Francaise Bunge (The Eastern City)* [1958] 2 LloydÑ Rep. 127

Lensen Shipping Co. Ltd v. *Anglo-Soviet Shipping Co., Ltd* (1935) 40 Com. Cas. 320; (1935) 52

Ll L Rep 141

Maintop Shipping Co. v. *Bulkindo Lines (The Marinicki)* [2003] 2 LloydÑ Rep. 655, see also

(The Dagmar) [1968] 2 LloydÑ Rep. 563

Markappa Inc. v. *N.W. Spratt & Son Ltd. (The Arta)* [1985] 1 Lloyd's Rep. 534.

Mediolanum Shipping Co. v. *Japan Lines Ltd (The Mediolanum)* [1984] 1 LloydÑ Rep. 136

Mediterranean Salvage & Towage Ltd v. *Seamar & Commerce & Inc.* (REBORN) [2008]

EWHC 1875 (comm)

Midwest Shipping v. *D.I. Henry (Jute)* [1971] 1 LloydÑ Rep. 375

Motor Oil Hellas (Corinth) Refineries v. *Shipping Corp. of India (The

Kanchenjunga)* [1990] 1 LloydÑ Rep. 391

Newa Line v. *Erechthion Shipping Co. S.A. (The Erechthion)* [1987] 2 LloydÑ Rep. 180

Ogden v. *Graham* [1861], 31 L.J.Q.B. 26; 41 Digest 522, 3503; 1 B & S 773

Paker v. Winlow (1857) 7 E & B 942

Palace Shipping v. *Gans Line* [1916] 1 K.B. 138

Portsmouth S. Co., Ltd v. *Liverpool & Glasgow Salvage Association* (1929) 34 Ll. Rep. 459

Prekookeanska Plovidba v. *Felstar Shipping Corp (The Carnival and The Danilovgrad)* [1992] 1

Lloyd's Rep. 449; [1994] 2 Lloyd's Rep. 14 (C.A.)

*Procter, **etc.,** Ltd.* v. *Oakwise S.S. Co.* [1926] 1 K.B. 244; 41 Digest 520, 3491

Reardon Smith Line v. *Australian Wheat Board (The Houston City)* [1954] 2 Lloyd's Rep. 148; [1956] 1 Lloyd's Rep. 1(C.A.)

Reardon Smith Line v. *Australian Wheat Board (1956) 1 Lloyd's Rep 1*

Renton v. *Palmyra* [1957] A.C. 149, pp.173-174

Royal Greek Government v. *Minister of Transport (The Ann Strathatos)* (1949) 83 Lloyd's Rep. 228

St Vincent Shipping Co. Ltd v. *Bock, Godeffroy & Co. (The Helen Miller)* [1980] 2 Lloyd's Rep. 95

Smith v. *Dart* (1884) 14 Q.B.D. 105

Strathlorne S.S. Co. v. *Andrew Weir & Co.* [1934] 40 Com. Cas. 168, 50 Ll.L.Rep. 185

Summer v. *Salford Corporation* [1943] A.C. 283, p.297

Tage Berglun v. *Montoro Shipping Corporation (The Dagmar)* [1968] 2 Lloyd's Rep. 563

The Aegean Sea [1998] 2 Lloyd's Rep. 39

The Athamas (owners) v. *Dig Vijay Cement Co. Ltd (The Athamas)* [1963] 1 Lloyd's Rep. 287 (C.A.)

The Carnival [1992] 1 Lloyd's Rep. 449; [1994] 2 Lloyd's Rep. 14 (C.A.)

The Chemical Venture [1993] 1 Lloyd's Rep. 508

The Count (2007) 1 Lloyd's Rep. 60

The Eastern City [1958] 2 Lloyd's Rep 127, p.131

The Evaggelos Th [1971] 2 Lloyd's Rep. 200

The Hermine [1979] 1 Lloyd's Rep. 212

The Kanchenjunga [1990] 1 Lloyd's Rep 391

The Khian Sea [1979] 1 Lloyd's Rep. 545 (C.A.)

The Marincki [2003] 2 Lloyd's Rep 655

The Mary Lou [1981] 2 Lloyd's Rep. 272, p.279

The Saga Cob [1992] 2 Lloyd's Rep. 545 (C. A.)

The Stork (1955) 2 QB 68

Transoceanic Petroleum Carriers v. *Cook Industries Inc. (The Mary Lou)* [1981] 2 Lloyd's Rep. 272, p.279

Uni-Ocean Lines Pte Limited v. *C-Trade S. A. (The Lucille)* [1984] 1 Lloyd's Rep. 244

Unitramp v. *Garnac Grain Co. Inc. (The Hermine)* [1979] 1 Lloyd's Rep. 212 (C. A.)

Vardinoyannis v. *The Egyptian General Petroleum Corporation (The Evaggelos Th)* [1971] 2 Lloyd's Rep. 200

Abbreviations

ASBA charter A type of standard voyage charterparty issued by ASBA (Association of Shipbrokers and Ag

Baltime The Baltic and International Maritime Conference Uniform Time Charter

COSWP Code of Safe Working Practice

GENCON General purpose charterparty published by BIMCO

IISTL the Institute of International Shipping and Trade Law, University of Wales, Swansea

IMO International Maritime Organization

ISM Code: International Safety Management Code

ISPS Code: International Shipping and Port Security Code

NYPE New York Produce Exchange Form Time Charter, issued by the Association of Ship Brokers and Agents (USA), Inc.

SOLAS International Convention for the Safety of Life at Sea

VLCC Very Large Crude Carrier. A deep draught vessels deadweight 160,000/319,999 Tonsdead weight

Chapter One

Introduction

1

Introduction

When a shipowner lets and a charterer hires a vessel, in the charterparty, paramount in the terms of the charter will be the obligation that the vessel shall proceed to a safe port if it is a port charter; likewise, that the vessel shall proceed to a safe berth in the case of a berth charter.[1] In the past, when litigation of disputes arose between the shipowner and the charterers as to the safety of the port or berth, there was a need for lengthy exploration for legal precedence amongst the large number of cases earlier before the courts. Fortunately, this need has been eliminated since the classic comprehensive definition of what is or is not a safe port was extracted from Sellers LJ definition: ÈA port will not be safe unless, in the relevant time, the particular ship can reach it, use it and return from it without, in the absence of some abnormal occurrence, being exposed to danger which cannot be avoided by good navigation and seamanship.Š[2] This means that, when the order was given, the port or place was prospectively safe for the vessel to get to, stay at as far as necessary, and in due course, leave. But if some unexpected and abnormal event should occur which creates conditions of unsafety so that the vessel is damaged or delayed, that contractual promise does not extend to making the charterer liable for any resulting loss or damage to the vessel.[3]

Many charterparties embrace express terms concerning the safety of the places to which the vessel is nominated. In such cases the charterer is obliged to send the vessel to a safe port or place. The promise is usually confirmed by the addition of the phrase ÈsafeŠ before the name of the place e.g. Èo one safe portŠ or Èone safe port VentspilsŠ.[4]

---

[1] *Unitramp v Garnac Grain Co Inc (The Hermine)* [1979] 1 LloydŇ Rep 212 (CA).
[2] Per Sellers LJ in *The Eastern City* [1958] 2 LloydŇ Rep 127, at p 131.
[3] *Kodros Shipping Corp of Monrovia v Empresa Cubana de Fletes (The Evia (No.2))* [1983] 1 A.C. 736.
[4] *Archimidis* (2007) 2 Ll Rep 101.

2

If, however, the charter provides for a nomination of a port, but is silent as to its safety, the law will usually imply such a promise of safety when the charterer is allowed to nominate one or more unnamed ports within a specified range, e.g. ȅone/two safe ports East Coast North AmericaŠ. The contrary is that the law will not usually imply the safety obligation term when the ship is ordered to a named port, e.g. ȅto KuwaitŠ, provided that the ȅsafeŠ term is absent. The reason for this that the owner is assumed to have the responsibility of ascertaining whether the ship can safely trade there.[5] If the charterer is subject to an express or implied term as to safety, along with the charterer ordering the ship to an unsafe port, then he would be in breach of the charterparty contract even though the charterer is not aware of the nature of the port being dangerous.[6] In some charters, such strict liability has been lowered by using less strict obligation, e.g. ȅexercising due diligenceŠ; therefore, the charterer may only be liable if he has not exercised due diligence to send the vessel to a safe port.[7] In practice, the obligation of the shipowner to bring the vessel to the specific place of discharge is qualified by the clause ȅso near thereto as she may safely getŠ.[8] The intention and the effect of this clause are to excuse the shipowner from his obligation to bring the vessel to the agreed place if he is prevented by an obstruction involving an unreasonable delay.[9]

In order to have the option to use the clause, the master must get within the ambit of the port in the sense of being in an area or zone within a range of proximity not beyond the reasonable contemplation of the parties as fair and reasonable men.[10] It must be one which is convenient to both the cargo-owner and shipowner.[11] In order to avoid any claim this may arise from the holder of bill of lading or the consignee. A war clause may be invoked in the charter because political unsafety is better dealt with by war clauses than by relying on the invoking of the safe port

---

[5] *Archimidis* (2007) 2 Ll Rep 101.
[6] *Lensen Shipping Co. Ltd* v *Anglo-Soviet Shipping Co. Ltd* (1935) 52 Ll L Rep 141.
[7] Clause 3 of the Shelltime 3. ȅCharterers shall exercise due diligence to ensure that the vessel is only employed between and at safe portsý Charterers shall not be deemed to warrant the safety of any portý and shall be under no liability in respect thereof except for loss or damage caused by their failure to exercise due diligence.Š
[8] Shellvoy 11.83, 86; Gencon 11.8-9/ 13-14
[9] S. Boyd, A. Burrows, D. Foxton, Scrutton on Charterparties and Bill of Lading (1996, Sweet & Maxwell), p.134
[10] *Athamas (Owners) v. Dig Vigay Cement Co. (The Athamas)* [1963] 1 LloydŇ Rep.287 (C.A.)
[11] *Renton v. Palmyra* [1957] A.C. 149, at pp.173-174

clauses, or by reinforcing a claim for breach of the safe port obligation.[12] An alternative way of presenting claims if the vessel has incurred damage caused by visiting unsafe port if the contract has express clause of ŁemploymentČ and indemnityŠ.[13]

It is not sufficient that the nominated port should be safe merely in its physical characteristics. It must also be legally or politically safe.[14] Also, the physical safety of a port involves consideration of the character of the particular vessel concerned.[15] Therefore, if the vessel, because of her size, requires the assistance of a tug to enter the port and a tug is not available, such a port is unsafe.[16] A port may be safe for one ship but unsafe for another, since the characteristics of a particular ship will be very relevant.[17] But it would seem that if the only dangers to which a properly manned and equipped vessel of the size and type (the particular ship) in question will be exposed are those which can be avoided by the exercise of ordinary reasonable care and skill, that port is not, as a matter of law, unsafe and the order to proceed to it would not therefore be regarded as a breach.[18] If the degree of skill required to avoid the danger is more than a reasonable degree, then the port may be unsafe.[19] Case law has shown us that ports are dangerous only if the danger is a common characteristic of the ports; therefore, if the danger is abnormal in its occurrence at the port, then the port is safe and not dangerous in a legal sense.[20]

It is well established that the port must not only be safe when the ship is ordered to it, but also safe when the ship arrives.[21] If the port becomes unsafe before arrival, the shipowner may require another port to be nominated.[22]

---

[12] D. Yates (ed.), Contracts for the Carriage of Goods by Land, Sea and Air (1993, LLP), p. 238
[13] H. Baker, P. David ŁThe politically unsafe portŠ LMCLQ p.112 at p.125.
[14] Ogden v Graham (1861) 1 B&S 773
[15] Per Paker L.J. in The Saga Cob [1992] 2 LloydŃ Rep. 545 (C.A.), at page 550
[16] Brostrom, A. & Son v. Dreyfus, L. & Co. (1932) 38 Com. Cas. 79.
[17] Brostrom, A. & Son v. Dreyfus, L. & Co. (1932)38 Com. Cas. 79.
[18] W. E. Astle, The Safe Port, (1986, Fariplay Publications), p. 4.
[19] Kristiandsands Tankrederi A.S. and Others v. Standard Tankers (Bahamas) Ltd. (The Polyglory) [1977] 2 LloydŃ Rep. 336.
[20] The Marincki [2003] 2 LloydŃ Rep 655.
[21] I. Carr, International Trade Law, (2005, Cavendish Publishing), p. 168.
[22] The Evia (No.2) (1981) 2 LloydŃ Rep. 367.

In order for the obstacle to render the port unsafe, having regard to the nature of the adventure and of the contract would involve unordinary delay.[23]Therefore, a temporary obstacle, e.g. neap tide,[24] will not render the port unsafe; to do so, the obstacle or danger must be operative for a period sufficient to frustrate the commercial object of the contract.[25]

To bear in mind, under time charter, if the state of unsafety occurred while the ship is alongside but still in time to avoid the danger by leaving, the charterer is said to be under an obligation to give order to evacuate the port and renominate a new safe port.[26] However, there is a distinction between the voyage charters and time charters in terms of renomination of a safe port; it is applicable to have a duty of renomination for a time charterer but this is not true for a voyage charter.[27] The reason for the distinction is that a time charterer is in control of the employment of the ship, whereas in the voyage charter the destination of the ship might be fixed from the beginning.[28]

At the time of giving the nomination order, the owner or the master is not obliged to accept the nomination immediately even though nomination seems to be lawful. While the nomination order is given, the master (also the shipowner) is not under immediate duty to accept the nomination as the master is allowed for a reasonable time to make his decision, despite the lawful state of the nomination.[29] Once the master discovers the unsafety of the port, the trigger of the right to decline can be activated, and he can insist upon a valid one.[30]

The charterer who names an unsafe port must indemnify the shipowner against the consequences;[31] the owner may recover damages for physical damage to the ship,[32] for delay

---

[23] *Knutsford S. S. Ltd. v. Tillmans & Co.* [1908] A.C. 406.
[24] *Aktieselskabet Wriksen v. Foy, Morgan & Co.* (1926) 25 Ll.L.R. 442.
[25] S. Boyd, A. Burrows, D. Foxton, Scrutton on Charterparties and Bill of Lading, (1996, Sweet & Maxwell), p.131.
[26] *The Evia (No.2)* [1982] 2 Lloyd's Rep.307 (H.L.), at p.320.
[27] *The Evia* [1983] 1 AC 736 at p. 757. (HL) at p.763.
[28] *The Evia* [1983] 1 AC 736 at p. 757. (HL) at p.763, Cited in C. Sun, "Nomination of Ports by the Voyage Charterers" (1993) 5 SACLJ 207, at 212.
[29] *Kuwait Petroleum Corp v I&D Oil Carriers Ltd (The Houda)* [1994] 2 Lloyd's Rep. 541, at p. 555.
[30] *Motor Oil Hellas (Corinth) Refineries v. Shipping Corp. of India (The Kanchenjunga)* [1990] 1 Lloyd's Rep. 391.
[31] *Lensen Shipping Co.. Ltd v. Anglo-Soviet Shipping Co., Ltd.* (1935) 40 Com. Cas 320. (C.A.).
[32] *Reardon Smith v. Australian Wheat Board* (1956) 1 Lloyd's Rep 1.

5

caused to the ship, [33]or for the cost of avoidance by, for example, being ordered to proceed to an alternative port.[34]

If, despite the fact that the unsafety of the port is obvious, the master still proceeds into the port, the resulting damage is deemed to be caused by the navigational decision, which act constitutes a *novus actus interveniens*, breaks the chain of causation and debars the shipowner from claiming damages.[35] However, if the master experiences a danger which is not obvious, if the danger is slight so that the master was positioned on the horns of a dilemma, whether he chose to proceed into the port and incur some slight damage or chose to frustrate the charterersÑcommercial prospective of the vessel by refusing to proceed, the masterÑ act may not constitute a *novus actus interveniens*.[36]

Traditionally, however, the courts refused to invoke the 1945 Act for contractual dispute cases, in order to make apportionment between the charterer and shipowner if both had contributed toward the negligence in performing their duties.[37] This is despite the fact in *Vesta v. Butcher*[38] it was held that, where a defendantÑ liability was the same both in tort of negligence and in contract, the 1945 Act applied.

The ISM codeÑ primary aim is to establish an international standard for safety management and operational standard. Suffice to say that its interest extends to assisting the master to take a correct decision as to whether he shall refuse the chartererÑ order and request a fresh one, or to proceed if the port is presumed safe[39]. Furthermore, it will require the master to keep evidence of all works and preparations prior to the decision made for port entry. In doing so, the court will have good evidence to whether the master has acted in a good manner or he is negligent in entering the port without taking the proper measures.

---

[33] *Ogden v. Graham* (1861) 1 B&S 773; *"The Count"* (2007) 1 LloydÑ Rep Plus 60.
[34] *Evans v. Bullock* (1877) 38 LT 34.
[35] *G.W. Grace & Co., Ltd. V. General Steam Navigation Co., Ltd* [1956] 2 K.B. 383.
[36] *The Stork* (1955) 2 QB 68.
[37] J. Cooke, T. Young, A. Taylor, J. Kimball, D. Martowski, L. Lambert, Voyage Charters, (2007, Informa), p.130.
[38] *Forsikringsaktieselskapet Vesta v. Butcher* [1986] 2 All E.R. 488, noted by L.J. Anderson [1987] 1 LMCLQ 10.
[39] P. Anderson, ISM Code: a practical guide to the legal and insurance implications (2005, LLP, 2nd Edit.)

The ISPS code has created a safeguard from terrorist attacks for ports and shipping, by implementing its procedures, uniting both the operation of ships, and ports individually and concurrently as partners.[40] It is believed that courts may also use the ISPS code to find out the negligence of the master from the incorrect implementation of the ISPS which may render the master negligent.

Finally, risk assessment is a useful tool which may be adopted practically by the ship's master as well as by the court in deciding the case. First, the author's opinion will be looking at the master's possible duty in using the risk assessment to clear up the doubt as to whether the port is safe or not. Secondly, the court may examine such duty to make it a tool in deciding the award of the case. The input of large amounts of information, e.g. ISM and ISPS codes, together with law cases, will create fundamental tools of risk assessment for the master aboard the vessel. It will also provide him with the means to make a quick, correct decision in order to avoid disputes between shipowner and charterers.

---

[40] B. Soyer, R. Williams, 'Potential Legal Ramifications of the International Ship and Port Facility Security (ISPS) Code on Maritime Law', 2005 LMCLQ. p.515.

Chapter Two

"What constitutes a safe port"

2.1 What is a safe port?

A requirement on the charterer to name a safe port or berth switches obligation of a safe port from shipowner to the charterer.[41] His nomination of a loading/unloading is taken to warrant that it is safe for the ship.[42]

The definition of port safety provided by Morris LJ in *The Stork*[43] was, as has been noted by some authors[44], quoted with approval by Sellers LJ in the Court of Appeal in *The Eastern City*[45] which concerned damage to the vessel consequent upon the charterer̈s orders for the vessel to proceed to the port of Mogador, Morocco. It is to be noted, however, that Sellers in approving the classic definition of Morris inserted the additional words Èwhich cannot be avoided by good navigation and seamanshipŠ after ÈdangerŠ in the second sentence of Morris̈ wording. The full text of Sellers̈comments (the classic definition) in that regard has become the measure of whether a port is safe which will,[46] of course, be familiar to all those concerned with charterparty law[47]:

> È A port will not be safe unless, in the relevant period of time, the particular ship can reach it, use it and return from it without, in the absence of some abnormal occurrence being exposed to danger which cannot be avoided by good navigation and seamanshiṕ Š[48]

---

[41] In *The Khian Sea* [1979] 1 Lloyd̈ Rep. 545 (C.A.), the Court of Appeal held that, although a port or berth was not necessarily unsafe just because a vessel might have to leave it on the approach of bad weather, for it to be safe there had to be (a) an adequate weather forecasting system, (b) adequate availability of pilots, (c) adequate weather searoom to maneuver and (d) an adequate system for ensuring that the searoom was always available.

[42] E. Gold, A. Chircop & H.M. Kindred, Maritime Law (2003; Canada; Irwin Law),p. 385

[43] *Compania Naviera Maropan S/A v. Bowaters Lloyd Pulp and Paper Mills Limited (The Stork)* [1955] 2 QB 68, at p. 131

[44] Refer to W.E. Astle, The Safe Port, (1986, Fairplay Publications) p.15; M. Holden, Paynes̈ Carriage of Goods by Sea, (1954, Butterworth); K. Michel, War, Terror and Carriage by Sea, (2003, LLP), p.499.

[45] *Leeds Shipping Co.* v. *Societe Francaise Bunge (The Eastern City)*, [1958] 2 Lloyd̈ Rep. 127, (C.A.)

[46] Bennett p.51

[47] W.E. Astle, The Safe Port, (1986, Fairplay Publications) p. 4

[48] *Leeds Shipping Co.* v. *Societe Francaise Bunge (The Eastern City)*, [1958] 2 Lloyd̈ Rep. 127, (C.A.) p.131.

9

This statement was affirmed by Roskill LJ[49] in the Court of Appeal in *The Hermine*.[50] But attention was drawn by Mustill J to the fact that points of law could arise which may not be covered by the general principles laid down by Sellers, and that it might then be helpful to consult the earlier authorities[51], although that the conclusion of the court on such points of law should be consistent with those general principles.[52] Therefore, it is important to pause at those elements of the general principles which are extracted from the above definition.

2.2 First: the "Relevant period of time"

From the definition, the ﬁrelevant period of timeﬂmentioned clearly covers the entire period during the vessel usage of the port from the moment of entry to the time of departure.[53] In fact, the prospective safety of the port is to be judged as at the time of the chartererﬁ order to it, according to The House of Lords in *The Evia (No.2)*.[54] Thus, an order given in February to load in the Great Lake in June would be unimpeachable, even though the approach is impossible at the date of the order.[55] Further, Baker[56], referring to the speeches of Lord Roskill or Lord Diplock, suggests that nothing supports the idea that the charterer need only exercise reasonable foreseeability when nominating a port. The promise is that the port will be safe when the ship has to use it. If, the port is in fact blocked to the ship of her size by, for example, a submerged

---

[49] As per Roskill LJ, *The Hermine* [1979] 1 Lloydﬁ Rep. 212, cited in M. Wilford, Time Charters (2003, London, LLP) p.193.

[50] *The Hermine* [1979] 1 Lloydﬁ Rep. 212 as per Roskill LJ remarked: ﬁy it is now quite unnecessary, in these unsafe port or unsafe berth cases, to refer back to the multitude of earlier decisionsý There is the law clearly stated. What has to be determined by the tribunal of fact in each case is whether, on the particular facts, the particular warranty of safety has or has not been broken.ﬂ

[51] See the earlier cases such as: ***Procter, etc., Ltd*** v. *Oakwise S.S. Co.*, [1926] 1 K.B. 244; 41 Digest 520, 3491; *Ogden* v. *Graham* [1861], 31 L.J.Q.B. 26; 41 Digest 522, 3503.

[52] M. Wilford, T. Coghlin & J.D. Kimball, Time Charters (2003, London, LLP) p.194.

[53] A.D. Hughes, Case Book on Carriage of Goods by Sea (Blackstone Press), p.26.

[54] *Kodros Shipping Corp. of Monrovia* v. *Empresa Cubana de Fletes (The Evia)* (No.2) [1983] 1 A.C. 736.

[55] C. Baker, ﬁThe safe port/berth obligation and employment and indemnity clausesﬂ (1988) LMCLQ p.43 add volume.

[56] C. Baker, ﬁThe safe port/berth obligation and employment and indemnity clausesﬂ (1988) LMCLQ p.43.

obstruction at the time the order is given, the port will be considered to be prospectively unsafe[57], even though the charterer or his agent are not aware of such obstruction.[58]

A charterer $\hat{N}$ primary duty as to the safety of a nominated port does not extend to supervening unsafety resulted by abnormal events.[59] In other words, a port is dangerous only if the danger is a usual characteristic of the port. Therefore, if the danger is an abnormal occurrence at the port (i.e. one which a reasonable person would not expect at that port), the port is not dangerous in the legal sense.[60] By way of contrast, prior to the ship $\hat{N}$ arrival, if the hidden obstruction occurs after the order is given, the time charterer is still obliged to take all measures to protect the ship from the new danger.[61] This second obligation does not take place if the charterer has no means of knowing the abnormal occurrence $\hat{N}$[62]

In *The Mary Lou*[63], carefully analysed by the authority and decided that a promise that the vessel would be trading only between safe ports was a promise that any port to which the vessel was ordered should actually be safe for her throughout the period of charter. At first, in *The Evia (No.2)*,[64] Goff J followed Mustill J whose analysis of the authority he assumed to be correct. However, the House of Lords overruled *The Mary Lou* and upheld the decision made by the Court of Appeal[65], thus, the majority had reversed Goff $\hat{N}$ decision. Therefore, the House of Lords decided that the safe port, regarded as a promise by the charterers at the time the order, was given prospectively safety, i.e., that when the ship arrived there she will be safe for her to approach, enter, use and depart from in the absence of some unexpected or abnormal event. It has been suggested[66] that actually, unsafety turned out not to be the test.

---

[57] H. Bennett, ÈSafe port ClausesŠ, Chapter 4 p. 61 of D. Thomas (ed.), Legal Issues Relating to Time Charterparties (2008, London, Informa).

[58] H. Bennett, ÈSafe port ClausesŠ, Chapter 4 p. 61 of D. Thomas (ed.), Legal Issues Relating to Time Charterparties (2008, London, Informa).

[59] J. Cooke, A. Taylor, T. Young, J. Kimball, D. Martowski & L. Lambert, Voyage Charters, (2002, Informa), p. 129; the same point raised in M. Davies &A. Dickey, Shipping Law, (LB), p.241.

[60] *The Evia* (No.2) [1983] 1 AC 736.

[61] C. Baker, ÈThe safe port/berth obligation and employment and indemnity clausesŠ (1988) LMCLQ p.43.

[62] This point to be discussed in different Chapter.

[63] *Transoceanic Petroleum Carriers v. Cook Industries Inc. (The Mary Lou)* [1981] 2 Lloyd $\hat{N}$ Rep. 272.

[64] [1981] 2 Lloyd $\hat{N}$ Rep.627.

[65] [1982] 1 Lloyd $\hat{N}$ Rep. 334.

[66] B.J. Davenport, ÈUnsafe Ports AgainŠ (1993) LMCLQ 150.

A case which is a good illustration of the safe port for a particular ship at all times or only at certain times, is *The Eastern City.*[67] The facts of this case were that the vessel was chartered for a winter voyage from ône or two safe ports in MoroccoÑto Japan. The charterers gave orders to the ship to load at Mogador, where she arrived and dropped her anchor on 26 December. Two days later, the weather deteriorated and the master was worried that the anchor was dragging and tried to pick up the anchor and sail. But the ship encountered a strong gust of wind which forced the ship to hit the rocks adjacent to the anchorage. It was held by the Court of Appeal[68] that the port was unsafe because, during winter, it was exposed to sudden southerly gales which could not be predicted and which were liable to cause the ship to drag her anchors in the unreliable holding ground of the restricted anchorage area.

Many ports around the world suffer from meteorological, tidal or other reasons. Ships may have to wait for sometime prior to making their entry into the port, this does not in itself make the port unsafe.[69] Regarding this matter, a fundamental point is drawn from Delvin J[70] ruling that Ħaw does not require the port to be safe at the very time of the vesselÑ arrival. Just as she may encounter wind and weather conditions which delay her on her voyage to the loading port, so she may encounter similar conditions which delay her entry into the port, and the charterer is no more responsible for the one than for the other.Š[71]

Indeed, the port can be safe even though the ship has to sail to sea for safety at certain times or even in certain circumstances. Another case that emphasises the essence of the above case is the *Smith* v. *Dart.*[72] The facts of this case state that the port of Burriana in Spain was ruled to be a safe loading port even though the vessel loaded alongside a road and had to keep up steam (engine on stand by) so as to be ready to put to sea for a period of time in certain weather conditions.

---

[67] *Leeds Shipping Co.* v. *Societe Francaise Bunge (The Eastern City),* [1958] 2 LloydŠ Rep. 127
[68] *Leeds Shipping Co.* v. *Societe Francaise Bunge (The Eastern City),* [1958] 2 LloydŠ Rep. 127.
[69] M. Wilford, T. Coghlin & J.D Kimball, Time Charters, (2003, LLP), p. 194
[70] Delvin J in *The Stork* [1954] 2 LloydŠ Rep. 397. at page 415.
[71] Delvin J in *The Stork* [1954] 2 LloydŠ Rep. 397, at page 415.
[72] *Smith* v. *Dart* (1884) 14 Q.B.D. 105.

2.2.1 Temporary dangers

It is an old establishment from the case law that a temporary obstacle such as a bar[73], or the riverŇ water being low[74], will not render the port unsafe. What if the ship cannot enter the port due to bad weather or the state of the tide? Purely, temporary dangers sometimes do not make a port unsafe. But still, temporary dangers may be the element of unsafety.[75] Thus the temporary failure or movement of navigation aids such as lights or navigation buoys resulting from bad weather, may render the port to be unsafe if, due to the temporary nature of the deficiency, the shipŇ master is unaware of the failure of navigation aids.[76] This is because what is shown on the charts is the contrary to the reality; that it is suggested is an entirely different matter.[77] The port is inherently unsafe due to the defects of its system; its safety depends on a system that ensures that soundings are regularly maintained and lights are always in position and lit.[78] Regarding the fact that the danger is very temporary may not enable the charterer to escape liability.[79] In this context, a storm which made the port of Mogador unsafe in *The Eastern City*[80] was of short duration. The court held that the port would not have been unsafe if it had been possible to recognise the likely onset of such conditions in advance and therefore enable the master to prepare his ship beforehand and to leave the port safely.[81]

Therefore, the temporary dangers is proposed that will not render a port unsafe is only true in a sense that the danger is known which will delay the ship in reaching the port. Otherwise remaining in the port or in leaving it; this will not make the port unsafe.[82]

---

[73] *Bastifell* v. **Llyd** (1862) 1 H. & C. 388; *Parker* v. *Winlow* (1857) 7 E. & B. 942.
[74] *Schilizzi* v. *Derry* (1855) 4 E. & B. 873.
[75] M. Maclachlan, The ShipŇ master business companion (2004, Nautical Institute), p.522.
[76] See the judgment of Mustill J. in *The Mary Lou* [1981] 2 LloydŇ Rep. 272, at page 279.
[77] This is true until the master has taken all the measures to find out any failure by his duty in taking risk management in the entire situation.
[78] C..J. Billington, ÈManaging Risk in PortsŠ, Chapter 4 of C. Paker, Managing Risk in Shipping (1999, The Nautical Institute), p.57.
[79] C. Baker, ÈThe safe port/berth obligation and employment and indemnity clausesŠ (1988) LMCLQ, p.43.
[80] *Leeds Shipping Co. v. Societe Francaise Bunge (The Eastern City)*, [1958] 2 LloydŇ Rep. 127, (C.A.).
[81] *Leeds Shipping Co. v. Societe Francaise Bunge (The Eastern City)*, [1958] 2 LloydŇ Rep. 127, p.133 (C.A.).
[82] M. Wilford, Time Charters (2003, London, LLP), p.194.

2.2.2 Delay

What would be the length of time of danger to consider the port as an unsafe port? From the case law, what seems the accepted view is that the period of time of such length as would frustrate the charter.[83] This view is strongly supported in *The Hermine*[84] case, she was ordered to load grain at Destrehan, which lies on the Mississippi about 140 miles from the open sea. After loading, the vessel was delayed for about 30 days, the majority of delay being due to insufficient water in the channel, and the remainder being the grounding of another ship in the channel. The owners claim that the port was unsafe. The test that followed was whether it was sufficient to frustrate the adventure in order to render the port unsafe which it was in this case, since the delay was only temporary.

In other words, delays caused by temporary danger or obstruction may, however, render a port unsafe if the delays are of sufficient duration. Accordingly, Lord Loreburn in *Knutsford* v. *Tillmans*[85] has commented that it "does not mean unsafe at the moment, but it means unsafe for the period which would involve inordinate delay."[86] It was held by the House of Lords[87] that the shipowner was not justified in discharging the cargo at an alternative port after three days delay on such a long voyage. Such an approach is to be adopted, for example, for low tides, encountered in the ordinary course of navigation.[88] Where if the charter include a provision provides that the port shall be one which the ship can reach at any tide, even then a low tide which may delay the ship would usually result in a liability to pay damages, rather than discharging elsewhere or render the port to be unsafe.[89] However, it does not follow that a port which is safe at the moment, may become dangerous at short notice is necessarily a safe port.[90]

---

[83] Voyage p. 127
[84] *Unitramp* v. *Garnac Grain Co. (The Hermine)* [1979] 1 Lloyd's Rep.212.
[85] *Knutsford* v. *Tillmans* [1908] A.C. 406.
[86] Ibid p.408.
[87] Ibid, p.408.
[88] Per Lord Blackburn in *Dahl* v. *Nelson* (1880) 6 App. Cas. 38, at p.51, cited in Martine Dockray, Cases and materials on the Carriage of Goods by Sea, p.129.
[89] See *Horsley* v. *Price* (1883) 11 Q.B.D. 244.
[90] *Johnston Bros* v. *Saxon Queen Steamship (The Saxon Queen)* (1913) 108 L. T. 465.

2.3 Second: "The particular ship"

Whether or not a port is õsafeÑis a question of fact depending on the circumstances of each case.[91] Consideration must be given to the type of vessel involved. Thus a port may be safe for one type of vessel but not for another. For example, where the deep draught of a 300,000 ton VLCC tanker is too deep to access many ports, other smaller ships with a smaller draught may be perfect.

It is postulated by Baker[92] that the fact that the different size or characteristics of the ship is not relevant. Therefore, the port must be safe for the particular ship to which the charterparty relates. Thus, in *Brostrom* v. *Dreyfus*[93], the owner chartered their vessel, the Sagoland, to discharge its cargo at more than one safe port. Subsequently, after discharging in Liverpool she was ordered for further discharge in Londonderry, Northern Ireland. However, owing to her size she was not able to navigate through the narrow channel without the assistance of a tug. No tug was available so Londonderry was held to be unsafe for that particular ship. The nearest available tugs were in Glasgow. Nowadays, some types of ships are equipped with bow thrusters allowing them to enter ports which other ships cannot do so without a pilot or tugs facilities.[94] This is to say that the old rule would not apply for some modern type of ships.

---

[91] Per Morris LJ in *Compania Naviera Maropan* v *Bowaters* [1955] 2 QB at p.105.

[92] C. Baker, ÈThe safe port/berth obligation and employment and indemnity clausesŠ (1988) LMCLQ at p.43.

[93] *Brostrom, A. & Son* v. *Dreyfus, L. & Co* (1932) 44Ll. L. Rep.136. (1932)38 Com. Cas. 79

[94] S. Mankabady concludes that ÈThere was a time when the size of the berths available in ports dictated the limits to which the size of ships could be increased, especially as far as their length and draught were concerned. Nowadays, the ships dictate the size of the berths.Š See S. Mankabady, ÈThe Concept of Safe PortŠ (1973-1974) 5 JML&C 633.

2.4 Third: "Reach it, use it and return from it"   physical

Lord Justice Sellers̃definition covers not merely the port itself: the vessel must be able to reach the port, use it and return from it. The definition obviously includes the approaches of the port. Seller LJ went on to say: ĺmost, if not all, navigable rivers, channels, ports, harbours and berths have some dangers from tides, currents, swells, banks, bars or revetments. Such dangers are frequently minimised by lights, buoys, signals, warnings and other aids to navigation and can normally be met and overcome by proper navigation and handling of a vessel in accordance with good seamanship.Š[95] ĺReach it, use it and return from itŠ are phrases expressing the entire period during which the vessel is using the port from the moment of entry to the time of departure. This may sometimes to be extended to risks encountered on the approach of ports or even sometimes it can be extended to cover the risks on the open sea. Thus in *The Sussex Oak*[96] time chartered to proceed to Hamburg. During the course of her passage up the Elbe, ice was encountered. The pilot nevertheless considered it safe to proceed. Further on *The Sussex Oak*[97] was halted by a large ice floe and as it was not possible for her to turn around, the vessel proceeded ahead and forced her way through the ice, sustaining damage. Devlin J held: ĖThe charterer does not guarantee that the most direct route or any particular route to the port is safe, but the voyage he orders must be one which an ordinarily prudent and skilful master can find a way of making in safety.Š[98] Furthermore, the port will be unsafe if the approach is such that the port cannot be reached safely without dismantling part of her structure[99], or if the vessel has to lighten some of her cargo to enter the port.[100] In *The Palace Shipping* v. *Gans Line* [101], there was a risk of attack by the German force which considered the port to be unsafe.[102]

---

[95]*Leeds Shipping Company, Ltd.* v *Societe Francaise Bunge* [1958] 2 Lloyd's Rep. 127 at p.131 (C.A.).
[96] *GW Grace & Co Ltd* v. *General Steam Navigation Co Ltd (The Sussex Oak)* [1950] 2 KB 383.
[97] *GW Grace & Co Ltd* v. *General Steam Navigation Co Ltd (The Sussex Oak)* [1950] 2 KB 383.
[98] *GW Grace & Co Ltd* v. *General Steam Navigation Co Ltd (The Sussex Oak)* [1950] 2 KB 383.
Ibid. at p.391 S. Girvin, Carriage of Goods by Sea, p.391.
[99] Re Goodbody and Balfour, Williamson (1899) 5 Com. Cas. 59.
[100] *Hall* v. *Paul* [1914] 19 Com. Cas. 384; M. Wilford, T. Coghlin, & J. Kimball, Time Charters, (2003, LLP), p.201.
[101] *Palace Shipping* v. *Gans Line* [1916] 1 K.B. 138 cited in Time Charters
[102] See *The Saga Cob* [1992] 2 Lloyd̃ Rep.545 (C.A.).

For the port to be used safely it must be physically safe in its location, size and layout. It is not enough for the port to be safe if the port becomes unsafe for the ship to remain. Referring to *The Saxon Queen*[103], it was employed under a time charter and the ship was ordered to Craster[104] in the United Kingdom which was safe to be entered. However, the port turned to be unsafe as the wind had altered the conditions and it was held that it was not a safe port.

2.4.1: Local warnings

As it has mentioned above regarding the physical safety of the port, it should be provided with adequate weather warning and other information concerning conditions at port. Thus, the port of Jakarta in *The Marinicki*[105] case demonstrates how important it is to identify that particular aspect of the port which renders it unsafe. Due to the fact that the port has no proper system for reporting caused the owner to be unable to establish the presence of the obstruction when the ship was ordered to proceed to discharge there, although, the court deemed, on balance, that it was an unforeseeable fortuity and the port was not unsafe simply because of the obstruction.

That said, the charterer was found liable because the shipowner showed that the port is unsafe because there was no proper system for monitoring the safety in entering the channel and warning system to warn vessels using the portÑ approaches. It is important to bear in mind that for the seamanship practice, the master is required at all times, especially in port, to take the initiative to seek for local information and forecasts.[106] For example, when bad weather or high swell is endemic, it is made clear to the master that he should keep a weather watch to provide information to ensure that his vessel could be made safe. Shipowner may argue the point that damage can be caused to the ship due to the absence of local warnings at the port of call. Such an

---

[103] *Johnson v. Saxon Queen Steamship (The Saxon Queen)* (1913) 108 L.T. 564.
[104] A small port on the coast of Northumberland.
[105] *Maintop Shipping Co. v. Bulkindo Lines (The Marinicki)* [2003] 2 LloydÑ Rep. 655; see also *(The Dagmar)* [1968] 2 LloydÑ Rep. 563.
[106] *Tage Berglun v. Montoro Shipping Corporation (The Dagmar)* [1968] 2 LloydÑ Rep. 563.

argument can be based on the fact that all ships trading the high seas are governed by SOLAS[107] regulations obliged to be equipped with meteorological forecast information systems which provide the master with the weather forecast and the condition of the sea.

2.4.2 Port set-up-Infrastructure and mooring facilities

Once the set-up of the port is found to be deficient that it is dangerous for the vessel when handled with reasonable care, then the charterer is in breach of his warranty and he is liable for damage attributed to the ship. To illustrate this proposition, ports have been deemed unsafe for reasons other than its geographical and meteorological characteristics[108], i.e. mooring buoy has been removed for repair together with a small part of the fender. Therefore, the port was held to be unsafe after damage was caused to the ship in northerly gale.[109] A further case which was significant in developing the doctrine of port safety was *Axel Brostrom & Son* v. *Louis Dreyfus & Co.*[110] the owner had to procure a tug from Glasgow to assist in and out of Londonderry. There was a claim to recover from the charterers the cost of tug assistance on ground that the port is not safe without the vessel requesting tug assistance. The arbitrator before the court awarded the owner for the tug expenditure. The award was upheld by the court.[111] The *Brothers Steamship Company Limited* v. *R. & W Paul Limited*[112] case gives another example of the port being unsafe on grounds that the vessel prior to entry was obliged to lighten some of her cargo by way of ship to ship discharge in order to enable her to safely navigate into the dockÑ approaches. Sankey J

---

[107] See chapter 2 of the ÈInternational Convention of Safety of Life at Sea 1974Š is the chief instrument by IMO (International Maritime Organization) enforced on 25th of May 1980. 146 contracting states have adopted.

[108] *Reardon Smith Line* v. *Australian Wheat Board (The Houston City)* [1956] 1 LloydÑ Rep. 1, cited in M. Wilford, T. Coghlin & J.D. Kimball, Time Charters (2003, LLP), p.198; (see also *The Carnival* [1992] 1 LloydÑ Rep. 449, [1994] 2 LloydÑ Rep. 14 (C.A.) where the ship was damaged by a defective fender).

[109] *Reardon Smith Line* v. *Australian Wheat Board (The Houston City)* [1956] 1 LloydÑ Rep. 1, cited in M. Wilford, T. Coghlin & J.D. Kimball, Time Charters (2003, LLP), p.198; (see also *The Carnival* [1992] 1 LloydÑ Rep. 449, [1994] 2 LloydÑ Rep. 14 (C.A.) where the ship was damaged by a defective fender).

[110] [1932] 44 Ll L Rep 136.

[111] The court has referred to *Alhambra* [1881] LR 6 PD 68. and *Goodbody* v. *Balfour Williamson* [1899] 5 Com. Cas. 59 [1932] 44 Ll L Rep 136 at p. 137.

[112] (1914) 19 Com. Cas. 384.

held in that regard: ÈA safe port means a port to which a vessel can get in laden as she is, and at which she can lie and discharge always afloat.Š[113]

Indeed, *The Carnival*[114] case is quite an interesting case. The defective fender at the berth was not just the defective fender which caused the port unsafe, it was a combination with premature passing of *The Carnival* which caused the *Danilovgrad* ship to surge and yaw that caused the damage when it came into contact with the fender. The court held that the fender was the effective cause of damage thence the safe port warranty was broken.

2.4.3 Navigational aids

The comments of Paker LJ[115] included the existence of efficient navigation aids, lights and buoyage systems which are to be regarded as factors of a safe port. Hence, the relevant aids should be adequate to neutralise obstructions or hazards, where the opposite of that would constitute a danger to navigation and render the port to be unsafe. Furthermore, he went on to say: Èý if a hazard is, for example, properly lighted but for some extraneous reason, e.g. because the power supply was suddenly cut byý it cannot in our judgment be said that the port was prospectively unsafe.Š[116]

2.4.4 Political unsafety

Although the reasons for the port to be illegally unsafe are usually those features that solely concern the marine characteristics of a port, e.g. default in navigation aids, undredged channels, unmarked wrecks or shallows, unavailable tugs or sea room to allow the ship to leave the port in case of adverse weather condition. It is nevertheless case law that a well-established port may be also unsafe because of the risk of war or even a political situation and therefore, obligation

---

[113] (1914) 19 Com. Cas. 384 at p.387.
[114] *The Carnival* [1992] 1 LloydÑ Rep. 449; [1994] 2 LloydÑ Rep. 14 (C.A.).
[115] Per Paker LJ in *The Saga Cob* [1992] 2 LloydÑ Rep. 545 (C.A.), at page 550; M. Wilford, T. Coghlin & J. Kimball, Time Charters, (2003, LLP).
[116] Per Paker LJ in *The Saga Cob* [1992] 2 LloydÑ Rep. 545 (C.A.) at page 550.

pertaining to political safety is also extended within the chartererŇ safe port obligation. This is to say that ľpolitical risksŠ might include: blockage, terrorism, outright warfare, and war. A real world example is the war that occurred in Georgia and rendered its territorial waters to be a war zone. Thus, any vessel calling at a port in Georgia may add an obligation on the charterer to send the ship to a safe port. If the nomination is to be made to a Georgian port, the shipownerŇ defence may be implied by the court at the absence of any express obligation.[117] This is similar to a case which is a good illustration of how the court rendered the port unsafe in a war zone and at the same time an example of implying the safe port warranty has been upheld in *The Evaggelos Th*[118] when no express obligation as to safety is included in the charterparty. A ship was chartered to trade in the Red Sea (which was, at the time, a war zone). A term regarding safety was implied in charter by the court.

2.5 Fourth: "Abnormal events"

It seems to be obvious that the safety of port obligation is at the time it is going to be used, rather than to its safety during the time of nomination. That is to say that the port must be prospectively safe in regard to its characteristics and must be, in the absence of some abnormal unexpected event, be safe for the ship at the time of her arrival there. The leading authority is *The Evia (No.2)*[119] case. In this case *The Evia* was chartered on a Baltime form. It included the express provision that ǎhe vessel to be employedý between good and safe portsý Ň

In March 1980, *The Evia* was ordered by the charterer to discharge in Basra. At this time, there was no doubt that Basra was unsafe or indeed likely to become unsafe in the foreseeable future. On 1 July 1980, she arrived in the Shatt-al-Arab river. Due to congestion, *The Evia* had to wait until 20 August to complete her discharge. On the same day, navigation on the Shatt-al-Arab river ceased due to the outbreak of hostilities between Iran and Iraq. An arbitrator held that the

---

[117] Unless if an exception clauses is added to the charter.
[118] *Vardinoyannis v. The Egyptian General Petroleum Corporation (The Evaggelos Th)* [1971] 2 LloydŇ Rep. 200, cited in K. Michel, War, Terror and Carriage by Sea (2004, LLP), p.509.
[119] *Kodros Shipping Corp of Monrovia* v. *Empresa Cubana de Fletes (The Evia (No.2))* [1981] 2 Lloyd's Rep. 613; [1982] 1 Lloyd's Rep. 334 (CA); [1983] 1 A.C. 736; [1982] 3 W.L.R. 637(HL).

chartered was not in breach of clause 2[120] of the charterparty and that it was frustrated as from 4 October. Goff J[121] held that clause 2 had been breached. He also agreed to the arbitration umpire that apart from that breach the charterparty would have been frustrated but held that the charterers were not allowed to rely on frustration as a defence to the shipowner's claim for hire because it was self-induced. The charterers' appeal was allowed by the Court of Appeal[122], holding the contrary view that there had been no breach of the charter clause 2, and upheld the arbitrator's award in such aspect. The court also held, in agreeing with the umpire and Goff J, that clause 21[123] of the charterparty relating to war risks, was not effective to exclude the operation of the doctrine of frustration. The lesson learned from *The Evia* that charterers will not be responsible for damage to the ship which is unrelated to the prevailing-abnormal-characteristics of a port.

In *The Mary Lou*[124], Mustill J suggested that an event was abnormal if not characteristic of the nominated port.[125] Further, referring to the words of Lord Roskill[126] in *The Evia* that the port is not 'inherently unsafe' which means any causes of damage do not arise from the qualities or attributes of the port itself. In the same case, Lord Denning has strongly supported Lord Roskill's dictum in stating that if the vessel suffers damage although the set-up of the port is good due to 'some isolated, abnormal or extraneous occurrence unconnected with the set-up then the charterer is not in breach of his warranty.'[127]

---

[120] 'The vessel to be employed in lawful trades for the carriage of lawful merchandise only between good and safe ports' Clause 2 of Baltime Charterparty.

[121] [1981] 2 Lloyd's Rep 613.

[122] [1982] 1 Lloyd's Rep 334 (CA), by a majority, Lord Denning MR and Sir Sebag Shaw, Ackner LJ dissenting.

[123] 21(A). The Vessel unless the consent of the Owners be first obtained not to be ordered nor continue to any place or on any voyage nor be used on any service which will bring her within a zone which is dangerous as the result of any actual or threatened act of war, war hostilities, warlike operations.

[124] *Transoceanic Petroleum Carriers* v. *Cook Industries Inc (The Mary Lou)* [1981] 2 Lloyd's Rep 272.

[125] *Transoceanic Petroleum Carriers* v. *Cook Industries Inc (The Mary Lou)* [1981] 2 Lloyd's Rep 272, at p. 278. cited H. Bennett, 'Safe ports and places', cited as Chapter 4 in D.R. Thomas (ed.) Legal Issues Relating to Time Charterparties, (2008,Informa), p.59.

[126] Per Lord Roskill in *The Evia (No.2)* [1982] 2 Lloyd's Rep. 307, at page 317.

[127] Per Lord Denning, MR in the Court of Appeal [1982] 1 Lloyd's Rep. 334, see fn. 57 the quote of Paker, LJ in *The Saga Cob* [1992] 2 Lloyd's Rep. 545, at page 550; cited M. Wilford, T. Coghlin, & J. Kimball, Time Charters, (2003, LLP), p. 201,p.200 delet

Referring again to *The Evia*, the House of Lords emphatically rejected the interpretation of safe port undertaken in regard to abnormal occurrence given by Goff J.[128] It is, therefore, believed that there is no extension of the primary promise of safety which does not extend to subsequent events that regarded as unexpected and abnormal even in case the characteristics of nominated port has been altered.[129] Regarding the above, it has been commented that ÈThe contrary view expressed at first instance was condemned as a (heresy)[130] and overruled.Š[131] A commentator from the essence of *The Lucille*[132] has concluded that if Èdamage has arisen from some different risk then the concept of abnormal occurrence might have been relevantŠ[133], but it can be concluded that if at the time the ship is ordered to the port it is unsafe due to risks caused by a certain situation, any subsequent increase in those risks, due for example a worsening of that situation, should not amount to abnormal occurrence.

2.6 Fifth: "Dangerous which cannot/can be avoided by good navigation and seamanship"

One of the most contested issues in the average unsafe port occurrences is when the vessel has been handled negligently by her master, pilot or crew. It is out of concern that the safety or lack of safety of the port if the major cause of the damage suffered by the ship is attributed to her own wrongful navigation or lack of good navigation and seamanship.[134] Up to this point, someone may wonder the level of ordinary good navigation and seamanship. It is believed that such facts may vary from one case to another. Practically speaking, prior to port arrival, preparation is part of ĝood navigation and seamanshipÑ which consists of identifying the prospective hazard, evaluating risks and deciding on a course of action to manage those risks.[135] Dangers which are

---

[128] Such interpretation was followed by Robert Goff in the Court of Appeal [1982] 1 LloydŇ Rep 334 at p.339; the analysis of abnormal events proffered by Mustill J in *The Mary Lou*, see fn. 65.

[129] H. Bennett, ÈSafe ports and placesŠ, cited as Chapter 4 in D.R. Thomas (ed.) Legal Issues Relating to Time Charterparties, (2008,Informa), p.60.

[130] *The Evia* [1983] 1 AC 736 at p.757 (HL).

[131] Op. Cit **fn**. 74.

[132] *Uni-Ocean Lines Pte Limited* v. *C-Trade S.A. (The Lucille)* [1984] 1 LloydŇ Rep. 244 cited in Keith Michel, War, Terror and Carriage by Sea,(2004,LLP), p.511.

[133] M. Wilford, T. Coghlin, & J. Kimball, Time Charters, (2003, LLP), p. 201.

[134] Time Charters p. 202

[135] It can be seen as comprising of five steps: 1. Identification of hazards; 2. Assessment of risks associated with these hazards. 3. Consideration of alternative ways of managing these risks; 4. Decisions

avoidable by those ordinary good navigation and seamanship measures will not render a port unsafe.

In *The Eastern City,* Sellers LJ said: ÈMost, if not all, navigable rivers, channels, ports, harbors and berths have some dangers... Such dangersý can normally be overcome by proper navigation and handling of a vessel in accordance with good seamanship.Š[136] But the port will be unsafe if the good seamanship required is more than the ordinary skill. The shipowner in *The Polyglory*[137] has settled a claim in respect of a damaged pipeline as a result of pilot negligence and sought to recover the amount from the charterers on the ground that the port of La Nouvelle was unsafe. The court upheld the arbitratorsÑaward and said the principle to be applied in deciding whether the port was unsafe, that if the vessel properly manned and equipped will be exposed to danger that can be avoided by Èthe exercising of ordinary reasonable care and skill that port is not, as a matter of law, unsafe and the order to proceed to it is not therefore a breachý Š[138] It is also held that the arbitrators were justified in finding the port unsafe because the dangers could only be avoided by very high standards of navigation and seamanship.[139]

In some cases, the court seems to rule in favour of the shipowner by giving some excuse to the negligence of the master or crew which they believed to be below the standard of the required good seamanship and practice to be exercised by them. This can be illustrated in *The Mary Lou*[140] as it has been pointed out that Èpossibility must be taken into account, namely that the casualty was the result of simple bad luck.Š[141]

---

on which option to select. For further information, see C. Billington, ÈManaging Risk in PortsŠ, as Chapter 4 in C.J. Parker, Managing Risk in Shipping (1999, Nautical Institute).

[136] Dictum of Lord Justice Morris in *Compania Naviera Maropan S/A* v. *Bowaters Lloyd Pulp and Paper Mills Ltd. (The Stork)*, [1955] 1 Lloyd's Rep. 349; [1955] 2 Q.B. 68.

[137] *Kristiandsands Tankeri* v. *Standard (Bahamas) (The Polyglory)* [1977] 2 LloydŇ Rep.353.

[138] Per Paker J in *Kristiandsands Tankeri* v. *Standard (Bahamas) (The Polyglory)* [1977] 2 LloydŇ Rep.353 at p.361.

[139] Per Paker J in *Kristiandsands Tankeri* v. *Standard (Bahamas) (The Polyglory)* [1977] 2 LloydŇ Rep.353 at p.361.

[140] *Transoceanic Petroleum Carriers* v. *Cook Industries Inc. (The Mary Lou)* [1981] 2 Lloyd's Rep. 272.

[141] Per Mustill J in *Transoceanic Petroleum Carriers* v. *Cook Industries Inc. (The Mary Lou)* [1981] 2 Lloyd's Rep. 272 at p.279.

Referring to *The Carnival*[142] case, a ship was moored when she was pressed by the negligent navigation of a passing ship into a defective fender on the berth which pierced her hull. In the Admiralty Court, Sheen̂ J[143] judgment was affirmed by the Court of Appeal.[144] The voyage charterer was held liable for their breach of safe berth obligation.[145] From this case it seems that negligent navigation by another ship which caused the immediate accident will not enable the charterer from his liability. It is now obvious that over the years there have been a large number of disputes between shipowners and charterers over questions of liability for damage suffered by the vessels; allegedly due to the berth or port being unsafe. Accordingly, there has been the need for an extensive exploration for legal precedence amongst several of the earlier cases before the courts.[146]

Refreshingly, this necessity has to a large extent been eliminated since the classic statement of Sellers LJ[147] about the state of the law with reference to the problem of the unsafe port, which leaves now for determination whether, on the facts of each individual case, the particular warranty of safety has been broken.[148] This may provide a well settled area of law by providing some valuable guidance as to matters which may render the port or berth unsafe within the meaning of the law.[149] Although, the courts must examine the characteristics of the vessel[150] and the port to determine whether the port or berth is unsafe, the examination of safety is a question of fact, but the criteria which has to be applied in determining whether the port is safe is a matter of law.[151] There is a considerable body of case law involving the meaning of the safe port before

---

[142] *Prekookeanska Plovidba* v. *Felstar Shipping Corp (The Carnival and The Danilovgrad)* [1992] 1 Lloyd's Rep. 449; Independent.

[143] *Prekookeanska Plovidba* v. *Felstar Shipping Corp (The Carnival and The Danilovgrad)* [1992] 1 Lloyd's Rep. 449; Independent.

[144] *Prekookeanska Plovidba* v. *Felstar Shipping Corp (The Carnival and The Danilovgrad)* [1994] 2 Lloyd's Rep. 14 (C.A.).

[145] As well as the passing ship for negligent navigation, contribution was then ordered between the two under the Civil Liability (Contribution) Act 1978.

[146] W. E. Astle, International Cargo Carriers liability, (1984, Fairplay Publications), p.131

[147] Refer to *The Eastern City* (1958).

[148] W.E. Astle, International Cargo Carriers liability, (1984, Fairplay Publications), p. 131.

[149] W.E. Astle, The Safe Port, (1986, Fairplay Publications), p.3.

[150] Seller LJ in *The Eastern City* also observed that the safety otherwise of a port was to be judged by reference to the particular chartered vessel assuming that it is Ëproperly manned and equipped, and navigated and handled without negligence and in accordance with good seamanship.Š

[151] Tony Schroder, ËUnsafe ports on account of iceŠ, the Swedish Club letter 2-2006.

The Eastern City case, but the latter has given a settlement on the law[152], yet any discussions about the warranty typically starts with an examination of its definition given by Sellers LJ.[153] Furthermore, Wilson commented saying that the case law suggests that the law in this area remains the same irrespective of type of charterers (time or voyage) or relates to an express or implied warranty.[154] As it has been discussed above, the scope of the port safety is the subject of considerable body of case law. However, Bennett[155] emphasising that the extract from the judgment of Seller LJ[156] is accepted as encapsulating the essence of the term Ìsafe portŠ which gave a steady settlement of law in this area. Even if there is a need of a new point of law on safe ports to be generated, it should be decided consistently with this dictum.[157]

---

[152] The definition of a safe port adopted by clause 2 of the charterparty Laytime definitions 1980 is clearly based on the SellerŃ LJ definition: Èý a port which during the relevant time a ship can reach, enter, remain at and depart from without, in the absence of some abnormal occurrence, being exposed to danger which cannot be avoided by good navigation and seamanship.Š

[153] N.J. Gaskell, C. Debattista & R. Swatton, Chorley & GilesŃShipping Law, (8th edn., Pitman Publishing), p.221.

[154] J.F. Wilson, Carriage of Goods by Sea, (1998, Pitman Publishing), p.26.

[155] H. Bennett, ÈSafe Port ClausesŠ, as chapter 4 of the D. R Thomas (ed), Legal issues relating to time charterparties, (2008, Informa), p.51.

[156] See the definition related to fn. 5 in the first chapter.

[157] *Transoceanic Petroleum Carriers* v. *Cook Industries Inc (The Mary Lou)* [1981] 2 LloydŃ Rep 272 at p.276.

Chapter Three

What is the difference between express and implied warranty of safety obligation?

3.1 Express warranty

The voyage or time charterers' right to nominate ports is usually paralleled with an express (warranty) obligation of nominating a safe port, e.g. Ène safe port VentspilsŠ.[158] The word ÈsafeŠ in this context refers not only to factors such as high winds, heavy sea, bad constructions of the jetty, dolphins[159], etc., but also to other factors such as warlike operations and political disturbances.[160]

The charterer is obliged to nominate, and in so doing, the charterer therefore warrants that the port or berth is safe.[161] This warranty may cover to some extent to the berths within the port. This means that the safety standard for a berth will be the same as that for a port. Some standard charter forms, for example, the Asbatankvoy[162] or Baltime 1939[163] provide: ÈThe vessel to be employed in lawful trades for the carriage of lawful merchandise only between good and safe ports or places where she can safely lie always afloat.Š[164]

The virtue of other clauses in charter may exclude the express warranty of safety, i.e. in Baltime[165] charter the effect of war risks clause which was intended to provide an exhaustive set of provisions to regulate the parties in the event of a nominated port becoming unsafe; this was held in *The Evia (No.2)*.[166] In contrast, in *The Chemical Venture*[167], the war risks clauses of the Shelltime 3 held to exclude the safe port warranty.

---

[158] *Archimidis* [2007] s Ll. Rep. 101. In such circumstances the charterer has promised that the port will be safe despite the fact that the port has been expressly identified.

[159] L. Gorton, R. Ihre, A. Sandevärn & P. Hellenius, Shipbroking and Chartering Practice, (1999, LLP), p. 223

[160] These last mentioned factors are often dealt with in a special war clause such as Barecon A, BIMCOŇ clause Voywar 1993, and GENCON charterparties.

[161] *Leeds Shipping Co. v. Societe Francaise Bunge* [1958] 2 LloydŇ Rep. 127 (C.A.) (voyage charters) and *Grace v. General S.N. Co.* [1950] 2 K.B. 383 (time charters).

[162] Clause 9 of Asbatankvoy.

[163] Clause 2 of the Baltime 1939.

[164] Clause 2 of the Baltime 1939 and Clause 9 of Asbatankvoy.

[165] Clause 21 in Baltime 1939 charter.

[166] *The Evia* (No.2) [1983] 1 AC 736, HL.

[167] [1993] 1 LloydŇ Rep 508, QB.

3.2 When does the implied warranty to be implied?

Some charters such as GENCOM form contain no express warranty. The question then arises whether, in the absence of an express warranty, is the court willing to imply a warranty? Where there is no express warranty of safety it seems that the court is in doubt of applying the warranty but it may in certain circumstances invoke the imply term of safety.

Although MorrisÑLJ dictum in *The Stork*[168] summarised that the implication is automatic in regard to the warranty of safety, it seems from the present trend of authority which gives each circumstance its own particular judgment depending upon the true construction of the charter. In the case of *The Aegean Sea*[169], for example, it was accepted that if the charter provides port nomination but still silent as to its safety, it may be that the warranty of safe port or berth will be implied, nevertheless, this is not always the situation in every case. In reference to Scrutton[170], if the charter provides for the ship to go to a named port or berth, or to one or more as ordered, but contains no provision as to safety, it would be doubtful whether the charterer will be under safety obligation thereof.

There are two situations that can be distinguished regarding the implication of safety[171]; the law will usually imply such a promise of safety when the charterer is allowed to nominate one or more unnamed ports within a specified range, e.g. Ène/two safe ports, East Coast, North AmericaŠ[172]; conversely, the law will not usually imply such a term when the ship is ordered to a named port, e.g. ĦHong KongŠ or possibly, to one or more ports out of a range of named ports, e.g. Ħo Southampton or to NewcastleŠ, the reason believed to be that the more specific the information given in the charter to the owner about the intended port, the more reasonable it is to

---

[168] *Compania Naviera Maropan SA* v. *Bowaters Lloyd Pulp & Paper Mills Ltd (The Stork)* [1955] 2 Q.B. 68, at p.105.
[169] *The Aegean Sea* [1998] 2 LloydÑ Rep 39.
[170] S. Boyd, A. Burrows & D. Foxton (Eds.), Scrutton on Charterparties and Bill of Lading, (London, Sweet & Maxwell), p.127
[171] J .H. S. Cooke, T. Young, A. Taylor, J. Kimball, D. Martowski & L. Lambert, Voyage Charters (2007, Informa Law).
[172] *The Evangelos Th* [1971] 2 LloydÑ Rep 200.

believe that the owner is satisfied with the safety of the port, or that he is prepared for the risk that it is unsafe.[173]

In the very recent case of *The Reborn*[174], the shipowner appealed and claimed for compensation for damage allegedly suffered by his vessel as a result of contact with an underwater object at the loading berth. The appeal was against the decision of an arbitrator that there was no absolute duty in the respondent charterers to nominate a safe loading berth. The vessel was chartered under GENCON form of voyage charter and the loading port being specially named as Chekka (there were several possible berths within the port to which the vessel could be directed). There was no express warranty to nominate a safe port or berth.[175] The appeal was dismissed on the grounds that there was no need, in term of business efficacy, to imply a warranty by the charterer that the berth would be prospectively safe due to the following reasons outlined by the court: first, the shipowner has agreed to load the vessel at the identified port of Chekka which means that he agreed to take the risk of any dangers in getting it, using it and departing from it. Second, the two provisions[176] in the charterparty meant that the owner had undertaken that the vessel would proceed to the nominated berth in Chekka or near it, and that obligation on the owner was not contingent on the vesselN safety. It is essential now to distinguish the three forms of contract.

Firstly, if the charter specifies the loading ports or places, and there is no express term in the charter as to the safety of ports similar to the one used in *The Houston City*[177] case, it would, therefore, be unnecessary to imply any undertaking on the part of the charterer that is safe, especially that the owner has not stipulated for an express warranty. He may be assumed to be content to bear the risk of unsafety himself. The same point was adapted by Mustill J in *The*

[173] See generally *Reardon Smith Line Ltd.* v. *Australian Wheat Board (The Houston City)* [1954] 2 LloydN Rep. 148 and *Atkins International* v. *Islamic Republic of Iran Shipping Lines (The A.P.J. Priti)* [1987] 2 LloydN Rep. 37, cited in J. Cooke, T. Young, A. Taylor, J. Kimball, D. Martowski & L. L.ambert Voyage Charters (2007, Informa) p. 112
[174] *Mediterranean Salvage & Towage Ltd* v. *Seamar & Commerce & Inc. (REBORN)* [2008] EWHC 1875 (comm).
[175] Clause 1 of the Gencon standard terms had been modified by the parties so as to delete the word ÈsafetyŠ in relation to proceeding to the loading port.
[176] Clause 20 and Clause 1 to be read together.
[177] See *Reardon Smith Line Ltd.* v. *Australian Wheat Board (The Houston City)* [1954] 2 LloydN Rep. 148

Helen Miller[178] where he stated that ÈWhere the charter-party expressly stipulates the place at which the vessel shall load or discharge, the shipowner is regarded as having consented to the risk that the place will prove to be unsafe.Š[179] However, Bennett arguing said that Èit seems strange and an unlikely interpretation of a contract, that a charterer should have the right to nominate a port that has become unsafe.Š[180] BennettÑ argument is believed to be true; the reason is that where the port is named, the owner has assumed the responsibility of ascertaining whether the ship can safely trade there.[181] Also the charterer unreasonably would compel the shipowner to choose between running the risk of damage and paying for that damage for breach of contract when the contract can be performed according to its provisions through another choice of named port that remains safe.

Secondly, the charterparty may leave the ports of loading/discharging to be nominated by the charterer, perhaps within a limited range, but which is not itself specified by name, e.g. Èone/two safe ports, East Coast, North AmericaŠ. Although the view from relying on cases such as *The Houston City*,[182] the warranty of the safe port would be believed to be implied. However, there is still a lack of direct authority on the question whether in such situation a warranty of safety should be implied.[183] In referring to *The Aegean Sea*[184], Thomas J was not prepared to accept that it was necessary to imply the warranty as he said: Èi do not think that one can conclude in general that a term as to safety will always be impliedÿ where there is an unspecified range of ports.Š[185] In contrast, a nomination of this type can be appreciated and the court in a time charter case was prepared to imply a term as to safety to give Ècommon sense and business efficacyŠ.[186] This has been stated by the words of Donald J in *The Evaggelos Th*[187], Èif I were faced with a

---

[178] *St Vincent Shipping Co* v. *Bock, Godeffroy & Co (The Helen Miller)* [1980] 2 Lloyd's Rep. 95
[179] *St Vincent Shipping Co* v. *Bock, Godeffroy & Co (The Helen Miller)* [1980] 2 Lloyd's Rep. 95 at p.101
[180] H. Bennett, ÈSafe Port ClausesŠ, cited as chapter 4 in D.R. Thomas, Legal Issues Relating to Time Charterparties, (2008, Informa), p.72.
[181] However, the situation is different when adjective ÈsafeŠ is added before the named port or place, e.g. Èone safe port Ventispils.Š In such circumstances the charterer has promised that the port will be safe despite the fact that the port has been expressly identified. See ÈArchimidisŠ [2007] 2 Ll. Rep.101.
[182] [1954] 2 LloydÑ Rep. 148.
[183] See *The Evaggelos Th* [1971] 2 LloydÑ Rep. 200, at p. 204 Donald J was under no doubt that a warranty should be implied.
[184] *Aegean Sea Traders Corp* v. *Repsol Petroleo SA (The Aegean Sea)* [1998] 2 Lloyd's Rep. 39.
[185] *Aegean Sea Traders Corp* v. *Repsol Petroleo SA (The Aegean Sea)* [1998] 2 Lloyd's Rep. 39. at p.68.
[186] *The Evaggelos Th* [1971] 2 LloydÑ Rep.200, at p.204
[187] *The Evaggelos Th* [1971] 2 LloydÑ Rep.200

simple charter which provided that the vessel was only to go to such port or place within a specified range as might be nominated by the charterý I should have no hesitation in implying a qualification that the port or place had to be safe.Š[188]

Thirdly, where the charters stipulate a nomination of a safe port, it would follow that the berth, docks, wharves and other places within the port to which the ship is directed must impliedly be safe. On the other hand, where chartererŇ obligation is to nominate a warranted safe berth at a named port, this brings with it no implication, at least as regards the approaches to the port, that the port is also safe. In other words, if the charterer is to nominate a Èsafe berthŠ at a named port (without specifying whether the port is to be ÈsafeŠ), the charterer has warranted the safety of the berth and its approaches but not the safety of the port as a whole or of the approaches to the port. The authority is found in *The APJ Priti*[189] case, the charter was for a voyage to È1/2 safe berths Bandar Abbas, ½ safe berths Bandar Bushire, ½ safe berths Bandar Khomeini in chartererŇ optionŠ and neither the port or its approaches in this case have their safety impliedly warranted. No argument was advanced that there was any implied safe port undertaking in respect of the nominating port of Bandar Khomeini, and it is clear that any such argument would have failed. However, the court went on to hold that Èthere will be no breach by the charterers even if a berth nominated is prospectively unsafe, if every berth or the port as a whole are prospectively unsafeŠ[190], but if the unsafety affects different parts of the port differently, then he may be in breach.

This was explained by Bingham LJ: Èwhere all the berths or ports as a whole are prospectively unsafe, the owners should not have agreed the discharge port in the first place or the master should have taken advantage of the clauses entitling him to discontinue the voyage.Š[191] It was also held by the Court of Appeal in *The APJ Priti* that the safe berth term in such charter could not be used to cover the safety of the approach to the port as opposed to movements within the

---

[188] *The Evaggelos Th* [1971] 2 LloydŇ Rep.200, at p.204
[189] *Atkins International* v. *Islamic Republic of Iran Shipping Lines (The APJ Priti)* [1987] 2 LloydŇ Rep. 37
[190] *Atkins International* v. *Islamic Republic of Iran Shipping Lines (The APJ Priti)* [1987] 2 LloydŇ Rep. 37 at p.42
[191] *Atkins International* v. *Islamic Republic of Iran Shipping Lines (The APJ Priti)* [1987] 2 LloydŇ Rep. 37 at p.42

port to and from a nominated berth.[192] The Court of Appeal is loath to imply the safety of port for two reasons: first, because such an implied term would not necessary be for the business efficacy of the charter; second, because such an implied term would at best lie uneasily beside the express terms of the charter."[193]

In the *The Erechthion*[194] case, it was held that the charterer may be held to be liable in relating to orders to an unsafe berth if either (a) in all circumstances the orders are regarded as those of the charterers and those orders are in breach of safe berth obligation (implied or express), or (b) the negligent act of the agent will render the charterer vicariously liable even if no implied or expressed of safety obligation is in the charter. This opinion has been raised in *The Mediolanum*[195] case.

3.3 Alternative wording or provision to lower level of scope of obligation

3.3.1 "Due diligence"

Although a safe port undertaking is a common feature in charterparties (especially time charter), some alternative wordings need to be incorporated into the charter in order to divert the strict liability port obligation to a lower level of scope of obligation on the part of the charterer. For example, clause 3 of the Shelltime 3 provides the follows: "Charterers shall exercise due diligence to ensure that the vessel is only employed between and at safe ports" Charterers shall not be deemed to warrant the safety of any port" and shall be under no liability in respect thereof except for loss or damage caused by their failure to exercise due diligence." The appliance of such a clause renders the charterers in breach if they have failed to take reasonable

---

[192] *Atkins International* v. *Islamic Republic of Iran Shipping Lines (The APJ Priti)* [1987] 2 Lloyd's Rep. 37 cited in M. Wilford, T. Coghlin & J.D. Kimball, Time Charters at p. 193
[193] *Atkins International* v. *Islamic Republic of Iran Shipping Lines (The APJ Priti)* [1987] 2 Lloyd's Rep. 37 (CA), at p.42
[194] *Newa Line* v. *Erechthion Shipping Co SA (The Erechthion)* [1987] 2 Lloyd's Rep. 180 cited in M. Wilford, Time Charters(2003, LLP), p.212
[195] *Mediolanum Shipping Co. v. Japan Lines Ltd. (The Mediolanum)* [1984] 1 Lloyd's Rep. 136

care in terms of a safe port or berth nomination. It has been suggested that a due diligence clause protects the charterer in circumstances where the charterer has not known or ought to know the circumstances which may cause the unsafety of the port or berth.[196] The test under clause 3 has raised an *obiter* comment of Paker LJ in *The Saga Cob*[197], that such clause may exonerate the charterer even in the case the port was prospectively unsafe.[198] He gave as an example the situation where a charterer who was unsure of the position enquired of a number of owners who used the port and was advised by all of them that the risk was so small that they would discount it.[199] In other words, the charterer should not be in breach of such a clause if they have made an enquiry in due diligence and come to a reasonable conclusion that the apparent danger does not amount to unsafety.[200]

In *The Chemical Venture*[201], the charterers were held in breach of their obligation of due diligence. The master of *The Chemical Venture* at first had refused to proceed to Mina Al Ahmadi during the Iraq/Iran war. The charterer persuaded the master to proceed by paying a war bonus. The ship has severely damaged by a missile in the channel leading to Mina Al Ahmadi with another three tankers in the previous eleven months. It was held by Gatehouse J that (a) the missile attacks by Iran was a normal characteristic of the port approaches; (b) the charterers, who knew the relevant facts, had failed to exercise due diligence and were in breach of Shelltime 3 clause 3.[202] In obligation of this type, the charterers delegated their right to nominate a port or berth to another, then due diligence must be exercised by others in making the nomination.[203]

---

[196] H. Bennett, ÈSafe Port ClausesŠ, cited as chapter 4 in D. R. Thomas, Legal Issues Relating to Time Charterparties, (2008, Informa), p.64.
[197] *The Saga Cob* [1992] 2 LloydÑ Rep 454.
[198] S. Baughen, Shipping Law (2004, Cavendish Publishing), p.210.
[199] The ruling judge went on to say that the absence of hostile attacks for eighteen months at the port was found not to be prospectively unsafe because the risk of guerrilla attacks was not a normal characteristic of the port. In ruling this, they reversed the lower courtÑ decision that the determination as to whether a guerrilla attack was a characteristic of the port was made on the basis of whether at the date the vessel was ordered there was a foreseeable risk of guerrilla attack.
[200] *The Saga Cob* [1992] 2 LloydÑ Rep 545 at p.551. (See B.J. Davenport, ÈUnsafe Ports Again: The Sage CobŠ, 1993 LMCLQ, p.150.
[201] *The Chemical Venture* [1993] 1 LloydÑ Rep. 508.
[202] Charterers shall exercise due diligence to ensure that the vessel is only employed between and at safe portsý Charterers shall not be deemed to warrant the safety of any portý and shall be under no liability in respect thereof except for loss or damage caused by their failure to exercise due diligence.
[203] J. Chuah, Law of International Trade, (2005, Sweet & Maxwell), p.280; the same point in find a safe loading place: due diligence cannot be delegated (Fairplay 1997, 331(5933), 18-19.

Furthermore, in *Dow Europe* v. *Novoklav Inc.*[204] held that due diligence in Shelltime 4 form was not to be construed to be referring to personal liability alone without clear words to the effect.[205] Although, in focusing of the words Ėdue diligenceŠ, Judge Diamond observed that such words have, in some occasions, protection to the charterer. ĖThe ownersý were inclined to submit that the qualification introduced by the wordsý confers no real protection on a charterer once a port is found to be unsafe. I do not entirely accept this.Š One may ask what then, according to the above quote of Diamond J, is the difference between the obligation of exercising due diligence and the obligation to nominate a safe port simpliciter?

Chong[206] suggests that the judge appears to have taken the view that the difference lies in the extent of knowledge of the prospective unsafety of loading or discharging at the port properly which is attributable to the charterer. Where the obligation of the charterer to nominate a safe port is qualified by the words Ėto exercise due diligenceŠ the knowledge concerning the prospective unsafety of the nominated port properly attributable to the charterer is that which his agents or servant knew or ought to know.[207] For this reason, many charterparties, particularly tanker charters, provide that the charterer is to be liable only if he has not exercised due diligence to send the vessel to a safe port or berth.[208]

---

[204] *Dow-Europe* v. *Novokla Inc* [1998] 1 LloydÑ Rep 306.
[205] See *Dow-Europe* v. *Novokla Inc.* [1998] 1 LloydÑ Rep 306, QB. Where chartererÑ duty is limited to one of due diligence, that duty will be regarded as non-delegable. Thus, in this case, the time charterer was held liable for the negligence of the port authority to whom they have delegated their duty of nominating a safe berth.
[206] D.G.S. Chong ĖRevisiting the Safe PortŠ (1992) SJLS 79, at p.96.
[207] H. Bennett, ĖSafe Port ClausesŠ, cited as chapter 4 in D.R.Thomas, Legal Issues Relating to Time Charterparties, (2008, Informa), p.67.
[208] See BPTIME clause 17.1 and BPVOY 4 clause 5.1: ĖBefore instructing Owners to direct the vessel to any port, charterers shall exercise due diligence to ascertain that the vessel can always lie safely afloat at such port but charterers do not warrant the safety of any port and shall be under no liability in respect thereof except for loss or damage caused by chartererÑ failure to exercise due diligence.Š

3.3.2 "So near thereto as she may safely get"

The intention and the effect of the term in GENCON[209] is to protect the owners against such hindrances that arise after fixture or negotiation and to excuse the shipowner from his obligation to bring the vessel to the agreed place if he is prevented by an obstruction involving an unreasonable delay.[210] A term such as ìso near thereto as she may safely getî[211] provides an alternative way of performance. It was held in the House of Lords in *Dahl* v. *Nelson*[212] that should the arrival, or cargo operation at port was prevented, the vessel is bound to wait for a reasonable time before adopting the alternative place of loading or discharging. The contrary was held in *Parker* v. *Winlow*[213], such a phrase held not to protect the shipowner when his vessel must to wait until the spring tides rather than divert the ship to another port as near thereto as she may safely get. Also, temporary obstructions such as low tide or high winds would not generally permit for an alternative performance or renomination of a port.[214]

Furthermore, in Scrutton, the reasonable time is suggested to be fixed by commercial considerations, and by the nature of the voyage performed.[215] The test whether the vessel has to reach a place close enough to come under the ìso nearî phrase is a port or a place which is reasonable and fair for reasonable men, also there is no absolute requirement that it must be the nearest apparent port or place.[216] It is a requirement to decide in light of the convenience of the cargo owner as well as the shipowner.[217] For example, in *The Athamas*[218] case, a vessel was chartered on the GENCON to carry cement to Phnom Penh. After discharging a part of the cargo

---

[209] Clause 1 section 2 reads: ìThis said vessel shall, as soon as her prior commitments have been completed, proceed to the loading port(s) or place(s) stated in **Box 1o** or so near thereto as she may safely get and lie always afloat,ý î

[210] S. Boyd, A. Burrows & D. Foxton (Eds.), Scrutton on Charterparties and Bill of Lading, (1996, Sweet & Maxwell) p.134.

[211] See Shellvoy 11.83, 86; Gencon 11.8-9/ 13-14.

[212] *Dahl* v. *Velson* (1880) 6 App. Cas.38 cited in Voyage charters. p.131.

[213] *Paker* v. *Winlow* (1857) 7 E. & B.942

[214] The obstacle preventing her from reaching the named port, dock or berth need not be physical. See *Reardon Smith Line* v. *Ministry of Agriculture* [1862] 1 Q.B. 42 at p.87, cited in Scrutton p.134.

[215] S. Boyd, A. Burrows & D. Foxton (Eds.), Scrutton on Charterparties and Bill of Lading (1996, Sweet & Maxwell), p.134.

[216] *The Athamas (owners)* v *Dig Vijay Cement Co. Ltd (The Athamas)* [1963] 1 LloydÑ Rep. 287 (C.A.)

[217] *Renton* v. *Palmyra* [1957] A.C. 149, at pp.173-174. (Although it was suggested in this case that the convenience of the consignee is not paramount).

[218] *The Athamas (owners)* v. *Dig Vigay Cement Co. (The Athamas)* [1963] 1 LloydÑ Rep.287 (C.A.)

at Siagon, the pilot refused to take her to Phnom Penh on the grounds that the depth of water was too shallow to enable her to navigate through the passage river. The ship accordingly discharged at Saigon which is 250 miles away from Phnom Penh. Held, the shipowners were permitted to discharge the whole cargo at Saigon and to recover the full freight for a two-port discharge.

The relevant law is set out in *The Varing* where Scrutton LJ said: ẽy then you are chartered to go to a discharging place and cannot get there, you are bound to wait a reasonable time before having recourse to the clause ẽor as near thereto as she can safely getẼ You cannot arrive and, when you find that you cannot get in on the exact day you desire, immediately go off to a place which you describe as ẽso near thereto as she can safely getẼ When a reasonable time has elapsed, and when there is no chance of you getting in to your discharging place within a reasonable time, the ship is at liberty to go to a reasonable discharging place -ẽas near thereto as she can safely getẼ and can call upon the consignee to take delivery at the substituted place.Ẽ[219]

There is a point of concern that, when judging whether a port is safe or unsafe, there will be a difference in situations between those cases where a vessel which was stipulated in the charterparty to trade to a certain berth or port and those cases where the vessel was stipulated to trade to a certain range. In the first case, an obligation on the port of the owner to find out in advance whether the ship can safely go to the port or the berth. In the latter case, the obligation relies on the charterer to nominate a suitable port or berth for her.[220]

There are two final points to be considered. First, notice must be given to the charterer and bill of lading holder once the shipowner is determined to invoke the contractual clause which gives him the liberty to discharge the goods somewhere else. It appears from dicta in *The Athamas*[221] that despite the fact no express requirement in the clause for any notice, but it would be sensible for the owner to notify the charterer where he wish to have his cargo taken. Although, there might be no breach of the charter if the owner does not give notification, he may not be indemnified for

---

[219] *Fornyade Rederiaktiebolaget Commercial* v *Blake & Co. (TheVaring)* (1931) 39 Ll. L. Rep. 205, [1931] P. 79, at p.87.
[220] L. Gorton, R. Ihre & A. Sandevärn & P. Hellenius, Shipbroking and Chartering Practice (1999, LLP), p. 224.
[221] *The Athamas (Owners)* v. *Dig Vigay Cement Co. (The Athamas)* [1963] 1 LloydẼ Rep.287 (C.A.).

his demurrage or damages claims caused by delay.[222] Second, charters should remember that if they order the vessel to an alternative port in compliance with a safe port clause, cargo owners may be able to sue on the bill of lading. This action usually is made against the shipowner who may claim for compensation from the charterer under the employment and indemnity (or in tanker charterparties - bills of lading and indemnity) clause.[223] Charterers may protect themselves by making sure that the bill of lading presented is to be signed by the master has a sufficiently wide clear scope to protect them from this situation.[224]

3.3.3 "War Clause"

Referring to *The Evia* case, it demonstrates the added provision of the war clause which regulates the partiesÑrights and obligations in the event of war to protect the charterer from a wide scope of the safe port obligation expressed or implied elsewhere in the charter. Baker suggests that clause 21(A) of the Baltime[225] form has been relied upon by owners either as alternative to, or to reinforce, a claim for breach of safe port obligation. An example can be found in *The Eugenia*[226] where the vessel was trapped for several weeks in the Suez Canal during the 1956 war. Her owner brought a claim against the charterer for breach of the safe port obligation. A claim would have encountered difficulties since the absence of the express order for the ship to proceed via the Suez Canal and the owner being well aware of the risk of closure at the time of fixing the charter. The charterer was held liable under clause 21(A) for allowing the ship to continue trading in a dangerous zone. In *The Evia*[227], the House of Lords held that the charterers were not in breach of clause 2 of Baltime (the safe port clause) because the war clause (clause 21) constituted a œcomplete codeÑfor war risks, and therefore overrode clause 2. Indeed, it is

---

[222] J. Cooke, T. Young, A. Taylor, J. Kimball, D. Martowski & L. Lambert, Voyage Charters (2007, Informa) p. 132.
[223] D. Yates (ed.), Contracts for the Carriage of Goods by Land, Sea and Air (1993, LLP), p. 230.
[224] H. Baker & P. David, ÈThe politically unsafe portŠ, (1986) L.M.A.C.L. p.112, at p.121.
[225] Baltime, clause 21(a): ÈThe vessel unless the consent of the owners be first obtained not to be ordered nor continue to any place or on any voyage nor be used on any service which will bring her within a zone which is dangerous as the result of any actual or threatened act of war, war hostilities, warlike operations, acts of piracy or of hostility or malicious damage against this or any other vessel or its own cargo by any personý Š
[226] [1963] 2 LloydÑ Rep. 381.
[227] *The Evia (No.2)* [1983] 1 A.C. 736.

believed that questions of political unsafety are better to be dealt by war clauses than relying on the invoking of the safe port clauses.[228]

3.3.4 "Employment and Indemnity"[229] provisions

In common law, whenever one person orders another to perform some act which is not manifestly tortious or unlawful, the person who gave the request comes under an implied undertaking to indemnify the other from the consequences of adhering. Thus, if the indemnity is not expressed, then it will be implied into the time charterparty under the English law.[230] For an indemnity claim to succeed there is no need for a breach of contract to be proved by the shipowner provided he is able to establish the effective cause of loss made by the masterś compliance to the chartererś order.[231]

In *The Erechthion*[232], the vessel struck an unmarked wreck while complying with an order to proceed to an anchorage in the Bonny River. The arbitrator had found that the charter contained no ḃmply or expressŚ warranty of safe port warranty, but held that the chartererś liable under the implied indemnity. It follows that the court had upheld the arbitration award after the chartererś appeal. The court decided that as the intention was that the ship should lighten at the anchorage by discharging part of her cargo, the order therefore purely comes under employment, not navigation. It is suggested that claims brought under ḃemployment and indemnityŚ are generally treated as an alternative way of presenting claims for loss and damage resulting from ownerś compliance with the chartererś orders to proceed to a port which is unsafe.[233] However,

---

[228] D. Yates (ed.), Contracts for the Carriage of Goods by Land, Sea and Air (1993, LLP), p. 238.
[229] A typical employment and indemnity clause will reads as follows: The captain (although appointed by the owner) shall be under the orders and direction of the charterer as regards employment, agency or other arrangements, and the charterer hereby agrees to indemnify the owners for all consequence or liability that may arise from the captainý complying with such orders or direction.
[230] *Strathlorne S.S. Co.* v. *Andrew Weir & Co.* [1934] 40 Com. Cas. 168, 50 Ll.L.Rep. 185 cited in C. Baker ḂThe safe port/berth obligation and employment and indemnity clausesŚ L.M.C.L.Q., p.43, at p.57.
[231] H. Baker & P. David ḂThe politically unsafe portŚ L.M.C.L. p.112 at p.126.
[232] *Newa Line* v *Erechthion Shipping Co SA (The Erechthion)* [1987] 2 Lloydś Rep. 180.
[233] C. Baker & P. David ḂThe politically unsafe portŚ L.M.C.L. p.112 at p.125.

there is strong judicial support in *The Ann Strathatos*[234] for the idea that such a clause is to be regarded independently from other provision when granting a remedy.

---

[234] *Royal Greek Government* v. *Minister of Transport (The Ann Strathatos)* (1949) 83 Lloyd's Rep. 228.

Chapter Four

Rights and obligations of charterers/shipowners: the difference between voyage and time charterers obligation in terms of port renomination

4.1 What is the difference between voyage and time charterers' obligation in terms of port renomination?

In general, the criteria applicable for the safe obligation in the case of voyage charters are applicable in time charters too. But in *The Evia (No.2)*[235] their Lordships, mindful of distinctions between the voyage charters and time charters concerning the renomination under voyage charters, declined to treat voyage charters as equal to time charters in terms of the secondary obligation should the nominated port became unsafe after nomination. The reason for the distinction is that whereas a time charterer is in control of the employment of the ship, in contrast the voyage charter destination of the ship is fixed from the beginning; either as a matter of fact or a matter of legal fiction.[236] Lord Roskill stated that "If there is a single loading or discharging port named in the voyage charterparty then, unless the charterparty specifically otherwise provides, a voyage charterer may not be able to order that ship elsewhere [and] if that port or those ports had originally been written into the charterparty, and the charterer then has no further right of nomination or renomination."[237]

Cooke et al (2007) describe the consequences of this conclusion as follows: "the vessel must encounter the danger or wait until that danger is passed or wait until an unreasonable period or frustration has elapsed or will inevitably elapse."[238] From Cooke's quotation, it is believed that the first alternative (encountering the danger) is one that the court would be reluctant to adopt. However, the second alternative when the owner is relieved of his obligation to proceed to the port by means of frustration the charterparty.[239] Although frustration is the doctrine that has been supported by many scholars[240], this seems an extreme result, especially where the cargo may be safely loaded/discharged at an alternative port within the range allowed by the charterparty. This

---

[235] *The Evia* [1983] 1 AC 736 at p. 757. (HL) at p.763.
[236] *The Evia* [1983] 1 AC 736 at p. 757. (HL) at p.763, cited in L.S. Chan, "Nomination of Ports by the Voyage Charterer" (1993) 5 SACLJ 207, at 212.
[237] Per Lord Roskill, *Kodros Shipping Corporation of Monrovia Appellants v Empresa Cubana de Fletes Respondents (The Evia (No. 2))* [1983] 1 AC 736, at p.763.
[238] J. Cooke, T. Young, A.Taylor, J. Kimball, D. Martowski & L. Lambert, Voyage Charters, (2007, 3rd edn., London, LLP), at 5.56.
[239] Frustration is not the concern in this book.
[240] See H. Bennett, "Safe Port Clauses" in D.R. Thomas, Legal Issues Relating to Time Charterparties, (2008, Informa). p.63.

41

decision was approved by the Privy Council in *The Teutonia*[241], the facts of the case stated that where the nominated discharging port became unsafe due to the outbreak of war and the charter was not frustrated, the owner is entitled to freight for the delivery at a nearby port selected by the owner, and within the range permissible by the charter. This case gives some right to renominate in the case of a voyage charter. However, in *The Evia (No.2)* the House of Lords was not supportive in dealing with *The Teutonia* as a reliable authority for the reason that Lord Roskill believed that the case was decided long before the doctrine of frustration assumed its modern form.[242]

Furthermore, unlike the voyage charter, in time charters it is clear that the charterer bears the cost of the delay due to the renomination. In a more recent case, *The Jasmine B*[243], Diamond J has denied any obligation to renominate in a voyage charterparty: In the absence of any special provision in a charter-party, the effect of the nomination of a loading or discharging port by the charterer is that the charter-party must thereafter be treated as if the nominated port had originally been written into the charter-party and that the charterer has neither the right nor the obligation to change that nomination.[244] The editors of Scrutton recognised that it has not been decided in the case of voyage charters whether the charterer has a secondary obligation to nominate a fresh safe port.[245] They believe that they thought that there would be more problems where the charterparty expressly names the loading and discharging ports. They further suggest that the secondary obligation can be imposed by conferring a liberty or deviation clause to change the port such as limiting the charterer to the substitution of a neighbouring and convenient port, or alternatively by requiring the charterer to exercise the liberty in a reasonable way.[246]

---

[241] *Duncan* v. *Koster (The Teutonia) (1872)* L.R. 4 P.C. 17.

[242] *The Evia* [1983] 1 A.C. 763 at p.765.

[243] *Bulk Shipping* v. *Ipco Trading S.A. (The Jasmine B)* [1992] 1 Lloyd's Rep. 39 (this case was not concerned with the safety or unsafety of ports. Nonetheless, in L.S. Chan, Nomination of Port by the Voyage Charterer, Vol. 5 SAcLJ (1993) 207, at p.214, it has been notified that there is no difference in principle where the port becomes unsafe after a valid nomination).

[244] *Bulk Shipping* v. *Ipco Trading S.A. (The Jasmine B)* [1992] 1 Lloyd's Rep. 39, at p.42.

[245] S. Boyd, A. Burrows & D. Foxton (Eds.), Scrutton on Charterparties and Bill of Lading (20th edn, 1996, Sweet & Maxwell), p.129.

[246] S. Boyd, A. Burrows & D. Foxton (Eds.), Scrutton on Charterparties and Bill of Lading (20th edn, 1996, Sweet & Maxwell), p.129.

It is always open to the party to agree an alternative loading or discharging port. This can be achieved by way of a special provision in the charterparty, for example, a war or ice clause, or the ìso near thereto as she may safely getŠ provision in the charter.[247] At first sight, it may seem rather problematic to impose liberty to change the port when there is no stipulation of express provision[248], because the discharge of cargo at a port other than that named in the bill of lading may be a breach of ownerÑ obligations to the bill of lading holder.[249] If the charterer ordered the vessel to an alternative port in compliance with the safe port clause under the liberty clause, cargo owners may be able to sue the shipowner on the bill of lading contracts[250], unless a bill of lading issued under the charter incorporates the terms of the charter or contains suitable liabilities. Still, it is in the hands of the shipowner to claim indemnity from the charterer under the employment and indemnity clause.[251]

Alternatively, the losses incurred by the shipowner in such situations might be recovered from the charterer by way of an implied indemnity, given that the losses flow directly from a choice made by the charterer.[252]

4.2 When does the time charterer's duty to renominate a safe port arise?

The charterer would fulfil his obligation in ordering the ship to a prospectively safe port, but if the port subsequently becomes unsafe while the ship is en route to it, the charterer must renominate an alternative port which is then prospectively safe.[253] If the state of unsafety occurs while the ship is alongside or at the port of loading or discharging, but while there is still time to avoid the danger by leaving, the charterer is under obligation to order the ship to leave and issue

---

[247] H. Baker & P. David, ÈThe Politically Unsafe PortŠ, LMCLQ, p.112. See Chapter 2.
[248] The shipowner must look to his indemnity clause if faced with unexpected liabilities, which, in effect, means that the shipowner, not the consignee, must take the risk of the inaccessibility or insolvency of the charterer.
[249] J. Cooke, T. Young, A. Taylor, J. Kimball, D. Martowski & L. Lambert, Voyage Charters, (2007, Informa), p.119.
[250] E.H. Ivamy, Payne & IvamyÑ Carriage of Good by Sea, (13th edn, Butterworth), p. 139.
[251] R. Grime, Shipping Law, (2nd edn, Sweet & Maxwell), p.149.
[252] S. Baughen, Shipping Law (2004, Cavendish Publishing), p.209.
[253] J, Wilson, Carriage of Goods by Sea, (1998, Pitman Publishing), p.29. Wilson has referred to *The Evia (No.2)* [1982] 2 LloydÑ Rep.307, at p. 310.

a fresh order to another prospectively safe port.[254] In contrast, if it is impossible for the ship to leave, then no further obligation is imposed on the charterer; this was held in *The Evia (No.2)*.[255] Furthermore, it was held that in a similar situation may not assist the owners in such case. This was because the events that caused the unsafety did not occur until after *The Evia* entered Basra, when an order to leave the port and proceed to another port could not have been effected owing to the outbreak of war, as she had finished discharging the day that the war started. There had therefore been no breach of the safe port warranty in the circumstances of the case.[256]

The contrary was held, that a new obligation did arise to *The Lucille*[257], discharged from the same port of Basra. The facts of this case are that on 20 September the ship was ordered to discharge. At that date, the port was prospectively unsafe due to the outbreak of war. Following that date, on 22 September the Shatt al Arab river was closed. The vessel was trapped after she had finished her discharging on 23 October. The closure was not regarded as a separate abnormal event for which the charterers were not to be responsible and it is linked to the order given on 20 September, when the charterer was aware of the state of war.

One may ask if the secondary obligation required the knowledge of the unsafety. In *The Evia*, the outbreak of war was sudden and it was not something that any charterer would know or ought to know. Wilford[258] suggests that Lord Muskill in *The Evia (No.2)* seems more consistent with the way he describes the obligation as arising only where the charterers become aware of the fact that a state of unsafety has arisen. However, the author is of the view that if the knowledge is the key to imposing the second application, it will eventually be essential for the court to decide whether actual knowledge is necessary. Or should the court impose some of the duty on the part of the master in advising the charterer of a new danger which makes the port unsafe? Some charters stipulate a duty on the shipmaster to brief the charterer on any occurrence which may

---

[254] *The Evia (No.2)* [1982] 2 Lloyd's Rep.307 (H.L.), at p. 310.
[255] *The Evia (No.2)* [1982] 2 Lloyd's Rep.307 (H.L.), at p.320. The facts of this case are that *The Evia* was trapped in the Shatt Al Arab river after the outbreak of war.
[256] *The Evia (No.2)* [1982] 2 Lloyd's Rep.307 (H.L.).
[257] *Uni-Ocean Lines Pte. Ltd. v. C-Trade S.A.* (1983) 1 Lloyd's Rep. 244.
[258] M. Wilford, Time Charters, (2003, LLP), p.205.

affect the safety of the ship and/or the crew.[259] Further, Bennett [260] suggests that the secondary obligation will be triggered not merely by the fact that the nominated port became unsafe but by the charterer's knowledge of that fact.

4.3 Under the owner's right to consider or reject the order, should the vessel proceed into an unsafe port?

At the time of giving the nomination order, the owner or the master is not obliged to accept the nomination immediately even though the nomination seems to be lawful. Thus, if the validity of the nomination is doubtful, the master is allowed a reasonable time[261] in order to study the matter by consulting charts and nautical books, and by referring to electronic appliances available to him to ascertain the validity of the nomination, that the port is safe for his ship to call. The authority is given by Millett LJ in *The Houda*[262] where he says: ÈThe authority established two propositions of general application: (1) the master's obligation on receipt of an order is not one of instant obedience but of reasonable conduct; and (2) not every delay constitutes a refusal to obey an order; only an unreasonable delay does so.Š[263]

Once the master took the measures in ascertaining the safety of the port, and he found it not prospectively safe, the trigger of the right to decline a nomination can be activated by the owner, who can insist upon a valid one.[264] A valid point has been suggested[265] that the mechanism of declining a nomination is the prospective unsafety rather than breach of a safe port undertaking. Otherwise, in case of a due diligence clause, a port can be prospectively unsafe but the

---

[259] See NYPE 46 (line 76); NYPE 93 (line 100), cited in H. Williams, Chartering Documents (1999, LLP), p.90. ÈThe principle of the master's duty overlaps with safe port obligations and often with other aspects of the parties'responsibilities under the charter if not negated by the express terms.Š
[260] H. Bennett, ÈSafe Port ClausesŠ, cited as Chapter 4 in D.R. Thomas, Legal Issues Relating to Time Charterparties, (2008, Informa), p.63.
[261] *Midwest Shipping* v. *D.I. Henry (Jute)* [1971] 1 Lloyd's Rep. 375.
[262] *Kuwait Petroleum Corp* v *I & D Oil Carriers Ltd (The Houda)* [1994] 2 Lloyd's Rep. 541.
[263] *Kuwait Petroleum Corp* v *I & D Oil Carriers Ltd (The Houda)* [1994] 2 Lloyd's Rep. 541, at p.555.
[264] *Motor Oil Hellas (Corinth) Refineries* v. *Shipping Corp. of India (The Kanchenjunga)* [1990] 1 Lloyd's Rep. 391.
[265] H. Bennett, ÈSafe Port ClausesŠ, cited as Chapter 4 in D.R. Thomas, Legal Issues Relating to Time Charterparties, (2008, Informa), p 74.

nomination was not negligent, which would oblige the shipowner to run the risk of unsafety.[266] It is also believed that the shipowner may refuse to obey the order in case of the express term that the vessel shall Ĥie always afloatŠ; even if the ship is set on her hull without any damage, the master/owner is entitled to refuse the order.[267] This is because the facts of unsafety operate as a limitation against the chartererŃ scope of right in nominating the port even if a due diligence clause is incorporated into the charterparties for the purpose of constraining the shipownerŃ right to seek for liability.[268] Liability for damages on the charterer is not limited to damage caused to the ship when calling in an unsafe port; it also includes indemnity for delay if the charterer fails to make a valid nomination or renomination within the reasonable time required.[269]

As we will discuss below, particularly *The Stork*[270] case, the compliance with an order to an unsafe port will not usually consist of *novus actus interveniens*; therefore, the chain of causation will not be broken. In other words, the owner will not lose his right to damage or loss due to delay. However, with full knowledge of the facts, the owner may lose his right to reject the invalid nomination if he complies with it thereafter. Referring to the example in *The Kanchenjunga*,[271] she was chartered to perform consecutive voyages from safe ports in the Arabian Gulf. She was ordered for loading in Kharg Island, which the owner knows not to be a safe port in that it was exposed to Iraqi air raids. Nonetheless, she entered the port and tendered notice of readiness. Shortly afterwards, there was an air raid and the master sailed away refusing to load there. The House of Lords held that the order to sail to Kharg Island was uncontractual and the owners were entitled to reject it.[272] But the owner, by electing to agree to load in Kharg

---

[266] Or maybe pay to the charterer loss or damage for the non-compliances.

[267] *Tregeglia* v. *Smiths Timber* (1896) 1 Com. Cas. 360. cited in Voyage Charters, p. 133.

[268] H. Bennett, ĖSafe port clausesŠ as chapter 4 in D.R. Thomas, Legal Issues Relating to Time Charterparties. (2008, Informa), p.74.

[269] *Ogden* v. *Graham* [1861] 1 B. & S. 773.

[270] *Compania Narviera Maropan S.A.* v. *Bowaters Lloyd Pulp and Paper Mills Ltd. (The Stork)* [1955] 2 Q.B. 68.

[271] *Motor Oil Hellas (Corinth) Refineries* v. *Shipping Corp. of India (The Kanchenjunga)* [1990] 1 LloydŃ Rep. 391.

[272] *Motor Oil Hellas (Corinth) Refineries* v. *Shipping Corp. of India (The Kanchenjunga)* [1990] 1 LloydŃ Rep. 391. at p.400.

Island, was waiving or abandoning their right to reject the nominations[273] and claim damages from the charterers for breach of contract.[274] It remains a problem which has not been dealt with in the court, whether the owner after rejecting the responded unsafe port order, still retains his liberty to take the vessel only so near thereto as she may safely get.[275] Also, the reasoning of the House of Lords in *The Evia (No.2)*[276] on the availability of the war clause liberty would support this view.[277]

4.4 Negligence on the part of the master or navigator

From the above discussion, we have seen how the charterer is liable for damage or loss attributed to his act in nominating an unsafe port or berth.[278] However, the pendulum may swing back in favour of the charterer. The charterer may be found not to be responsible for the damage.[279] If the master, in fact, takes the vessel there and in doing so causes the vessel to become damaged, his liability will depend on whether or not he acted reasonably in the circumstances.[280] His knowledge of the port at that particular stage is important. If the danger of the port is obvious, if knowing that the port is unsafe, he still insists on proceeding and the vessel is damaged in consequence, his decision to obey the order would amount to a *novus actus interveniens* which breaks the chain of causation and debars the right of the shipowners to sue for the damage caused.[281]

---

[273] *Motor Oil Hellas (Corinth) Refineries* v. *Shipping Corp. of India (The Kanchenjunga)* [1990] 1 Lloyd's Rep. 391. at p.400.
[274] Some scholars believe that where the owner has no way in knowing the unsafety until the ship's arrival, then the master allowed rejecting the order because his conduct prior to arrival will create a bar to reject the order. See S. Mankabady, 'The Concept of Safe Port' (1973) 5 J. Mar. L. & Com. 633 1973-1974.
[275] See chapter 2 section 2.3.2.
[276] [1983] 1 A.C. 736.
[277] *The Evia (No.2)* [1983] A.C. 736 cited in J. Cooke, T. Young, A. Taylor, J. Kimball, D. Martowski & L. Lambert, Voyage Charters, (2007, Informa), p.134.
[278] *Portsmouth S. Co. Ltd* v. *Liverpool & Glasgow Salvage Association* (1929) 34 Ll. Rep. 459.
[279] *Larrinaga* v *The King* (1944) 78 LL. Rep 167.
[280] *Compania Naviera Maropan S.S.* v. *Bowaters Lloyd Pulp and Paper Mills Ltd. (The Stork)*[1955] 2 Q.B. 68, Per Singleton J. at p.89 the same point was raised in the judgment of Delvin J in the same case at p. 77.
[281] Girvin, p.260.

The test would appear to be this: if the master's obedience, though deliberate, was lawful, reasonable and free from blame[282] and if what he was doing was merely what an intelligent observer, knowing exactly how he was circumstanced, would have expected him to do[283], then any damage resulting would be the direct and natural consequences[284] of the breach of contract in giving the order. However, if the danger is not obvious and is slight, so that the master is placed on what is called the thorns of a dilemma– whether to proceed onto the port and incur some slight damage or to refuse to proceed[285] μ then, if the master's act was to proceed, doing so may not constitute a *novus actus interveniens,* and thereby the shipowner's right to claim damage is preserved.[286] This discussion was brought in *The Stork*[287] judgment that the master is sometimes on the horns of a dilemma. The material question isý whether he acted reasonably. The judge was of the opinion that the master, in accepting the assurances given to him, acted reasonably.[288]

The contrary was held when the matter was brought earlier in *The Houston City.*[289] Although Geraldton port was held to be unsafe due to two facts: (a) the absence of hauling off buoy; and (b) a missing section of fender on the wharf where the ship was berthed, when the ship sustained damage during a storm the dissenting judgment dealt with the argument that the master's act constituted a *novus actus interveniens* in the decision of the master to rely upon the fine weather and not to put out stream anchor intervened[290] which broke the chain of causation.[291] In such

---

[282] Per Lord Wright in *Summer* v. *Salford Corporation* [1943] A.C. 283, p.296 - 297.

[283] Per Lord Wright in *Summer* v. *Salford Corporation* [1943] A.C. 283, p. 297.

[284] Per Lord Wright in *Summer* v. *Salford Corporation* [1943] A.C. 283, p. 297.

[285] Thereby refusing to proceed may frustrate the charterers' commercial expectations of the vessel.

[286] *Compania Narviera Maropan S.A.* v. *Bowaters Lloyd Pulp and Paper Mills Ltd. (The Stork)* [1955] 2 Q.B. 68.

[287] *Compania Narviera Maropan S.A.* v. *Bowaters Lloyd Pulp and Paper Mills Ltd. (The Stork)* [1955] 2 Q.B. 68.

[288] Per Singleton J in *Compania Narviera Maropan S.A.* v. *Bowaters Lloyd Pulp and Paper Mills Ltd. (The Stork) [1955]* 2 Q.B. 68, at p. 68.

[289] *Reardon Smith Line* v *Australian Wheat Board* [1954] 2 Lloyd's Rep. 148.

[290] Per Dixon CJ in the High Court of Australia. *Reardon Smith Line* v *Australian Wheat Board* [1954] 2 Lloyd's Rep. 148, at p.158.

[291] Claims from loss or damage to the chartered vessel brought by the shipowner against the charterer are not claims for which the right of limitation is given by the 1957 or 1976 Limitation Conventions. Therefore, there is no limitation in the liability for such claims.

cases, the loss or damage is not the order of the charterer but the fault or neglect of the ownersÑ own servant in failing to perform his duty.[292]

Someone may ask how negligent must the master be before his acts are considered as eclipsing the charterersÑnomination of unsafe port as the effective cause of the damage. It is believed that the question in each case is whether the master acted reasonably in all the circumstances. A similar question arose in *The Arta*,[293] where the answer concluded by Ackner LJ as Ëhe modern tendency is in the direction of making *novus actus interveniens* depend to a large extent on the reasonableness of the intervening conductý however, the *novus actus* is that of the plaintiff himself, the same considerations applyý , principally whether his act is so unreasonable as to eclipse the defendantÑ wrongdoing.Š[294] It is believed that London arbitrators required a high degree of Ëutterly unreasonableŠ[295] conduct by the master to break the chain of causation; perhaps the mere negligence in itself does not provide the necessary very high degree of unreasonable conduct.[296]

Furthermore, if an unsafe place is nominated the master is not bound to take his vessel there; accordingly the master is generally given the benefit of the doubt when he is placed on the thorns of a dilemmaÑas to whether or not to proceed. In a previous case, the House of Lords[297] held that a well-drafted clause such as Clause 20(b)(vi)[298] of the ASBA charter gives the master the separate and independent right to refuse to proceed and that if he exercised such right, that would also protect the owner even if they had agreed to proceed.

---

[292] The same point was raised in *Larrinaga* v *the King* (1944) 78 LL. Rep. 167.
[293] *Markappa Inc.* v *N.W. Spratt & Son Ltd (The Arta)* [1985] 1 Lloyd's Rep. 534.
[294] *Markappa Inc.* v *N.W. Spratt & Son Ltd (The Arta)* [1985] 1 Lloyd's Rep. 534, p. 537.
[295] Per Waller LJ in *Emeh* v. *Kensington & Chelsea & Westminster Area Health Authority* [1985] Q.B. 1012.
[296] *Markappa Inc.* v. *N.W. Spratt & Son Ltd (The Arta)* [1985] 1 LloydÑ Rep. 435, at p. 537.
[297] *The Kanchenjunga* (1990) 1 Ll. Rep. 391.
[298] ËIf owing to war etcý entry to any such port of loading or dischargingý Be considered by the master or owners in his or their discretion dangerousý for the vessel to reachý Š

4.5 Contributory negligence

According to the above discussion, the chartererŇ liability under the express safe port clause is absolute. Also, if the express obligation of safe port or berth is absent and the port or berth is not specifically named, an implied contractual obligation may take place. However, in *Vesta* v. *Butcher*[299], Hobhouse J held after he had reviewed the authority that, where a defendantŇ liability was the same both in tort of negligence and in contract, the 1945 Act applied. [300] Thus, there is no solid reason for the Law Reform (Contributory Negligence) Act 1945 not to have application, especially in the case of implied obligation, which is believed to be less strict than the absolute duty under the expressed obligation.[301] This also applies to those under charterparties such as Shellvoy 2,[302] which expressly imposes on charterers a duty merely to use due diligence to ascertain that a port is safe.

In civil law countries, the law has followed a new trend toward finding fault on both sides; arbitrators and judges apportion the liability by applying a similar concept of the Contributory Negligence Act. The issue can be referred to the American case *Nassau Sand & Gravel Co. v. Red Star Towing & Transportation Co.*[303]; the argument was whether the owner would be concurrently liable because of the masterŇ questionable reliance on the chartererŇ port captainŇ assurance that the berth was safe. It has been stated that if the express assurance was received by the master that the berth was safe and relies on the assurance, then the owner is not liable. However, if the express assurance of berth has been received by the master and he does not rely on it and he negligently determines the depth to be safe and causes damage to the ship, such damages are proportioned between the owner and charterer. A commentator[304] argues that the

---

[299] *Forsikringsaktieselskapet Vesta* v. *Butcher* [1986] 2 All E.R. 488, noted by L.J. Anderson [1987] 1 LMCLQ 10.
[300] C. Baker, ÈThe safe port/berth obligation and employment and indemnity clauses, LMCLQ p.43, at p. 56
[301] See chapter 2.
[302] It merely imposes on charterers a duty merely to use due diligence to ascertain that a port is safe. Noted by C. Baker, ÈThe safe port/berth obligation and employment and indemnity clausesŠ,[1988] LMCLQ 43.
[303] 62 F.2d 356, 1933 AMC 54 (2d Cir. 1932), cited in Peter Hartman ÈSafe Port/Berth Clauses: Warranty or Due Diligence? 21 TML J 540 1996-1997.
[304] C. Baker, ÈThe safe port/berth obligation and employment and indemnity clausesŠ, LMCLQ p.43 at p. 55.

English court and arbitration can follow a similar path in adopting the apportionment idea via a different path, namely causation, such as a negligent act of the ship. Indeed, this is true in most cases. In 1974, Brabin J decided that the 1945 Act can be invoked when the contractual obligation in question is not absolute, but merely imposes a duty of reasonable care[305], although the courts (as in the example in *A.B. Marintrans* v. *Comet Shipping Co. Ltd.*)[306] traditionally refused to invoke the 1945 Act for contractual dispute cases.[307]

---

[305] *De Meza* v. *Apple* [1974] 1 Lloyd's Rep. 508.
[306] Per Neill LJ *A.B. Marintrans* v. *Comet Shipping Co. Ltd.* [1985] 1 W.L.R. 1270.
[307] J. Cooke, T. Young, A. Taylor, J. Kimball, D. Martowski, & L. Lambert, Voyage Charters, (2007, Informa), p.130.

Chapter Five

The Role and Relevance of International Codes and
Regulations in Ascertaining a Safe Port

5.1 How useful are the International Codes (ISM, ISPS) and regulations (risk assessment) to the master in determining whether a port is a safe port?

From the previous chapters, for the charterer to escape liability in event of an unsafe port, he has to show that the damage to the vessel was caused solely by the negligence of the master or crew or even by their contribution (*novus actus* **interveniens**). It has been stated that the master may sometimes be placed in the ãhorns of a dilemmaÑ mainly because of an initial breach of contract by the charterer as to the unsafe port in deciding whether to proceed into the port and guess that the ship may not get damaged or at the very least incur some slight damage, or to refuse to proceed and thereby frustrate the charterers commercial expectations of the vessel.[308] One may ask what would be the courtÑ gauge in deciding whether the action of the master constitutes negligence which breaks the chain of the causation of the chartererÑ negligence. In order to look into the answer, two factors will be discussed.

5.2 First: How can the ISM code to be used by the tribunal in order to evaluate the liability?

In the light of AndersonÑ suggestion[309], the master has several duties under the ISM code: to prepare prior to the entry the port, conduct a thorough examination by going through a checklist[310] to identify any unforeseeable hazards or dangers which may render the port to be unsafe. By doing so, the master will retain the evidence (either written in the logbooks or stored in the electronic equipment). As a natural consequence of the proper implementation to the ISM code prior to the port of entry, there will be a considerable amount of documentary evidence. The

---

[308] *Compania Naviera Maropan S.A.* v. *Bowaters Lloyd Pulp and Paper Mills Ltd. (The Stork)* (1955) 2 QB 68.

[309] P. Anderson, ISM Code: a practical guide to the legal and insurance implications (2005, LLP, 2nd Edn.), p. 89, the same point raised in the ISM Code Section 5: The MasterÑ responsibility and authority.

[310] P. Anderson, ÈThe Errors of Our Ways!Š 2007 MRI, Vol. 21; ISSU 2, pp. 16-17; p.3. What the company requires of its masters and bridge officers with regard to navigation and collision avoidance will be set out in its ãBridge Procedures ManualsÑor similar titled section of its SMS (ISM) procedures - possibly along with checklists and circulars - possibly with cross references to standard industry publications such as the Nautical Institute ãBridge Team ManagementÑor ICS ãBridge Procedures GuideÑ or similar for a safe port entry.

tribunal or court may use such evidence to provide an analysis of how and what went wrong by the action of the master or crew, or by the lack of preparation prior to the port which showed the non-implementation of the ISM code. This evidence will draw the attention of the tribunal or court to figure out the causal chain which leads to an accident, i.e. breach of ISM or other regulations.

Where the evidence indicates a breach of the master's duty, it will lead to a break in the chain of causation, and in such cases the cause of the loss or liability may not be the order of the charterer but the fault or neglect of the master in failing to perform his duty of implementing the ISM. In the hands of a claimant or prosecutor such documentary evidence could prove total devastation to the shipowner's defence.[311] It has been suggested that even if the danger of the port was not obvious, the adherence to the ISM recommendations will assist the master to take a correct decision whether to refuse the charterer's order and request a fresh one, or to proceed if the port is presumably safe.[312] Commentators[313] concluded that the evidence from implementing the ISM code, and the expectation of the existence of that evidence, does have an affect on the outcome of liability case, It also may make the difference between distinguishing simple negligence of a master from a more significant status of incompetence Although, the writer is in agreement that the ISM code is the gate which leads to discover the shipowner's mistakes committed by his master or crew, and that such a mistake again is likely to lead to either negligence or incompetence of the crew. Both lead to prejudice the owner from his right to claim.

5.3 Second, How can the ISPS code be used judicially to uncover the shipowner's negligence?

Increasingly, new situations arise in which it is difficult for a master to judge whether a port is safe. In the modern era, one such problem is terrorism. Terrorist attacks, directly or obliquely,

---

[311] P. Anderson, ISM Code: a practical guide to the legal and insurance implications (2005, LLP, 2nd edn.),

[312] P. Anderson, ISM Code: a practical guide to the legal and insurance implications (2005, LLP, 2nd edn.)

[313] Phil Anderson, Session 5 ISM and ISPS Codes - Influence on the Evolution of Liabilities, International Colloquium on Maritime Legal Liabilities (14-15 September 2006) in The Institute of International Shipping and Trade Law, University of Wales, Swansea, p. 5.

affect the safety of the ports around the world. But it is often difficult to assess whether the criminal violent activity carried out consists of civil war or terrorist activities? There is no black or white answer[314] but in marine industry and marine insurance matters it is usual to handle the matter that a terrorist is a person or group who will Ëy kill, maim and destroy for the sake of doing soý It is still, however, a public cause for concern and this separates it from other criminals who do things for their own gain.Š[315] One may ask why is it relevant to the topic of the safe port? The reason is that in order to avoid the likelihood of terrorist attacks, the ISPS Code lays down prevention procedures which may gear up the shipowner or the master with a safeguard against any attack at any port.[316] Indeed, the law regarding the terrorist attack is an area open for a possible conflict between the shipowner and the charterer. Such a problem can be raised in two possible circumstances. First, if the ÈwarŠ is not defined in the charter, the English courts adopt a commercial approach to define the war similar to the definition adapted in *Kawasaki Kisen Kabushiki of Kobe* v *Bantham SS Co. Ltd.*[317] The definition does not seem to give the term ÈwarŠ a wide meaning to extend it to the terrorist attack as it is described above.[318] It is because of this that many charterparties adopted a wider definition to the term war which extends it to the terrorist attack such as ShellLNGTime 1[319] charterparty or clause 35 of Shelltime 4. From the owner prospective, this can provide a useful protection.[320] Gardner[321]

---

[314] David Gardner, ÈTerrorist Attacks - Being PreparedŠ, (December, 2005) p. 1, cited as electronic article in Curtis, Davis & Garrard law firm site: http://www.cdg.co.uk/articles_view.php?pid=12&action= VIEW& news _id=88 &type_id=4

[315] M.D. Miller, Marine War Risks (LloydÑ of London Press Ltd, 2nd Edn.), p.193. cited in David Gardner, ÈTerrorist Attacks - Being PreparedŠ, (December, 2005) p. 1, cited as electronic article in Curtis, Davis & Garrard law firm site: http://www.cdg.co.uk/articles_view.php?pid=12&action= VIEW& news _id=88 &type_id=4

[316] E. Katarelos & A. Alexopoulos, ÈThe MasterÑ Role in Relation to the Safety of the Port, particularly under the Concept of the ISM and the ISPS CodesŠ, electronic articles cited in www.martrans.org:8093/symposium/papers/ Track%20B/B23%20katarelos%20et%20al.pdf

[317] Per Sir Wilfrid Greene MR in *Kawasaki Kisen Kabushiki of Kobe* v *Bantham SS Co. Ltd* [1939] 2 K.B. 544 Ël have no doubt that a captain of a tramp steamer arriving at Shanghai and finding the state of things described by the umpire would have no difficulty in recognising that a state of war existed.Š

[318] David Gardner, ÈTerrorist Attacks - Being PreparedŠ, (December, 2005) p. 1, cited as electronic article in Curtis, Davis & Garrard law firm site: http://www.cdg.co.uk/articles_view.php?pid=12&action=VIEW&news_id=88& type_id=4.

[319] Ëy blockage, war, hostilities, warlike operations, civil war, civil commotions, revolutions, acts of piracy, acts of terrorism, acts of hostility or malicious damage.Š

[320] David Gardner, ÈTerrorist Attacks - Being PreparedŠ (December, 2005), electronic article from Curtis, Davis & Garrard.

[321] David Gardner, ÈTerrorist Attacks - Being PreparedŠ (December, 2005), electronic article from Curtis, Davis & Garrard, p.1

suggests that whilst it may be impossible to trade ships in complete safety, the impact of any terrorist attack can be minimised if the issue is properly addressed by many tools such as the ISPS code at the time when the charterer is concluded and throughout the charter period. The ISPS code has created a safeguard to ports and shipping from terrorist attacks by implementing its procedures, where it embraces both the operation of ships, and ports individually and concurrently as partners.[322]

The author is in agreement that the ISPS code can be used as a hypothetical test which may place the owners in breach of the ISPS code if they fail to fulfil their duty under the code. One of the owner's duty is to check either directly or by reference the available databases and to decide whether or not the port is indeed ISPS compliant.[323] Hence, courts adopting the test of ISPS duty may render the master's incorrect compliance to the ISPS code and subsequently may procure a breach of the master's duty under the ISPS. Consequently, this may result in breaking the chain of causation rendering the shipowner negligent. This test might be applied throughout the proceeding voyage, prior to entry and whilst in a port. Furthermore, the court may refer to the professional judgement of the master in taking decisions in order to maintain proper security levels of the vessel.[324] Where there are contrary decisions by the master, these can infer as violating the ISPS code.

5.4 Risk assessment

Both the ISM and ISPS codes can be used as tools to explore the situation of the port whether it is safe or not to enter. The matter of concern is open for the court to adopt the method of risk assessment tests. If the judge sees that the master has carried out risk assessment properly in order to broadcast the safety and security levels of the port, the master, thereby, in so doing has

---

[322] B. Soyer & R. Williams, ËPotential Legal Ramifications of the International Ship and Port Facility Security (ISPS) Code on Maritime LawŠ, 2005 LMCLQ, p.515.

[323] B. Soyer & R. Williams, ËPotential Legal Ramifications of the International Ship and Port Facility Security (ISPS) Code on Maritime LawŠ, 2005 LMCLQ, p.515 at p. 517.

[324] E. Katarelos & A. Alexopoulos, ËThe Master's Role in Relation to the Safety of the Port, particularly under the Concept of the ISM and the ISPS CodesŠ, electronic articles cited in www.martrans.org:8093/symposium/papers/ Track%20B/B23%20katarelos%20et%20al.pdf

believed to be fulfilling his duties which render him not to be negligent. In view of the fact that if the risk assessment is carried out by the master, it will avoid many disputes between the charterers and shipowners[325] and "indeed prevent an incident occurring which may disrupt the smooth running of the ship."[326] It is widely known that the risk assessment tool can be brought into play to minimise risk from entering an unsafe port.[327] It would therefore, be apparent to the court that the master and the ship's crew carried the risk assessment from the way they implemented it and applied the ISM and ISPS in their practice. In this regard, lawyers should also review the industrial content such as risk assessment as this is mandatory by SOLAS and COWSP before an arbitration tribunal to identify precisely the causes of a dispute. Anderson suggests that prior to a formal court hearing, it may be appropriate for the judge to appoint an expert in ISM code or an expert in risk assessment to give advice to the disputing parties.[328]

Although, risk assessment practice took a different form in Code of Safe Working Practice and SOLAS, it is open for the user (ship's master) to adopt his company or his own formal procedures, as long as it will assist the master to determine whether the port is safe or not also, it can be the tribunal in making the correct judgment of the safe port. This section of the paper provides an easy form of risk assessment procedures, (see the risk assessment flow chart) using the contribution of ISPS code, ISM code, in addition to the court decisions from previous case law. All together they will form a fundamental risk assessment mechanism to determine whether the nominating port is a safe port or not.

---

[325] The Oil Companies International Marine Forum, Tanker management and self assessment: A best-practice guide for ship operators (2004, Witherby & Co. Ltd, 1st edn.), pp..28-29.
[326] Expert advice and consultancy listed in specialist firm on ISM and risk assessment (consultISM) site, on: www.Consultism.co.uk/client.html.charterers.
[327] B. Soyer & R. Williams, "Potential Legal Ramifications of the International Ship and Port Facility Security (ISPS) Code on Maritime Law", 2005 LMCLQ. p.515, at p. 517.
[328] Phil Anderson, paper on "ISM and ISPS Codes - Influence on the Evolution of Liabilities", International Colloquium on Maritime Legal Liabilities (14-15 September 2006) in The Institute of International Shipping and Trade Law, University of Wales, Swansea. p.10.

5.4.1 Risk assessment in practice

It was noted that risk assessment is important in the obligation of nominating a safe port.[329] The flow chart describes all the necessary phases and critical factors that the prudent master must be aware of.[330] Shipmasters must follow the charts and steps that will lead him to make the right decision on whether the port is safe to enter. The case table contains the abstracts of the most relevant law cases which can be selected by key words. Those cases are to be used along with the ISPS and ISM codes recommendations and guidance which will result in a good risk assessment tool.

5.4.2 How does the risk assessment's flow chart work according to each phase?

From the risk assessment flowchart, the phases are as the follows[331]:

Prior to signing the contract: The shipowner or master in consulting the risk assessment flowchart and once it is obvious that the charterer has breached the implied or express term of safety, they may refuse the order of the charterer.

When the contract is concluded: In the absence of the express obligation of nominating a safe port in the charter, the common law may imply an obligation of safety.[332] The obligation of a safe port has to be, in absence of some abnormal event, safe for the vessel at the time when proceeding normally, she can arrive at and remain at the port in due course.[333] Then the master does not need to comply with the order and request for a new legitimate order.[334] Following the authority from the ISM code, the master is the only person who is given the authority to make a decision in respect of the safety of the vessel: By the master has the overriding authority and the

---

[329] A. Manadaraka-Sheppard, Modern Maritime Law and Risk Management, (2007, Cavendish Publishing), p. 1025.
[330] E. Katarelos & A. Alexopoulos, ÈThe MasterÑ Role in Relation to the Safety of the Port, particularly under the Concept of the ISM and the ISPS CodesŠ, p.3.
[331] For a better understanding, study the provided chart along with this paper.
[332] *The Aegean Sea* [1998] 2 LloydÑ Rep 39. This matter has been discussed in chapter 2.
[333] *The Evia (No.2)* [1982] 2 LloydÑ Rep 307.
[334] It has been discussed in section 3.3

responsibility to make decisions with respect to safety and pollution prevention and to request the companyÑ assistance as may be necessary.Ŝ[335]

1. *Approaching the port*: if the master exercises the risk assessment flowchart and discovers that the port or terminal has subsequently become unsafe, the charterer is required to issue a fresh order to send the vessel to a safe port.[336] Moreover, if the master on arrival has discovered any hazards that render the port unsafe, he is still entitled to refuse to enter.[337]

2. *Period when the vessel at the port*: In point of fact, the safety obligation of the port is of concern at the time when the vessel is at the port rather than its safety at the nomination time.[338] Further to the discussion in chapter 1, the port must be physically safe in its layout, location, infrastructure and size for a particular ship to use at any relevant time, having regard to both its natural and artificial aspects.[339] The master and/or the shipowner may consult the risk assessment flowchart at the convenient stage on the chart. Accordingly, if in port the ship has faced subsequent events that render the port unsafe, and if the danger can be avoided by leaving, the immediate duty is to give orders to leave the unsafe port. However, this is only if the vessel can escape danger or damage. In *The Evia (No.2)*, no new obligation arose because by the time the war broke out, it was too late for the ship to leave the port and thereby avoid the danger.[340]

---

[335] ISM code: ðMasterÑ responsibility and authorityÑ section 5, p.4. The role of shipmaster is explained by Christopher Hill: ÈThe master of a ship is a man of many parts. He needs to be part disciplinarian, part accountant, part lawyer and more than part seaman/navigator. Above all, perhaps he needs to command the respect of his fellow men. He needs to have more than a fair measure of self-confidence and an ability to make a cool and rational judgement, sometimes at very short notice, in times of crisis. He is a servant in law, an agent both for his principal, the shipowner, and to some extent the owner of the goods he is carrying if his ship is under charter in respect of the employment of vessel. He is also a commander of men, his crew, and he occupies a position of special trust, a fiduciary relationship with his owner, he is absolutely responsible for the safety of his ship and remains in command regardless of whether or not his ship is in charge of a pilot at any given time.Ŝ Maritime Law (1995, LLP), p.495.
[336] See Section 3.3
[337] *The Kanchenjunga* [1990] 1 LloydÑ Rep 391.
[338] *The Evia (No.2)* [1982] 2 LloydÑ Rep 307. The same point in E. Katarelos & A. Alexopoulos, ÈThe MasterÑ Role in Relation to the Safety of the Port, particularly under the concept of the ISM and the ISPS CodesŜ, p. 4.
[339] *Johnson* v. *Saxon Queen Steamship (The Saxon Queen)* (1913) 108 L.T. 564.
[340] *The Evia (No.2)* [1983] 2 LloydÑ Rep. 307.

Although the law regarding the safe port obligation is a settled area, it is believed that still some risks of disputes between charterers and shipowners will be occurred, i.e. unsafe port due to terrorist attacks. Risk assessment tools can be brought into practice to minimise such risks. As many companies are now obtaining professional advice[341] and resolving disputes in making their own tailor-made tables or flowcharts risk assessment.[342] Consequently, assessment of risk can become a popular technique used by the master to provide him with an appropriate action plan as experts in this matter believe that risk assessment can and will be capable of reducing the exposure of several risks to ships.[343]

---

[341] ConsultISM is one of the suitable experts to give a professional advice in risk assessment. www.consultism.co.uk.
[342] A. Mandaraka-Sheppard, Modern Admiralty Law, (2001, Cavendish Publishing), p 959
[343] A. Mandaraka-Sheppard, Modern Admiralty Law, (2001, Cavendish Publishing), p.964

Risk assessment flowchart
Safe Port obligation's Criteria[344]

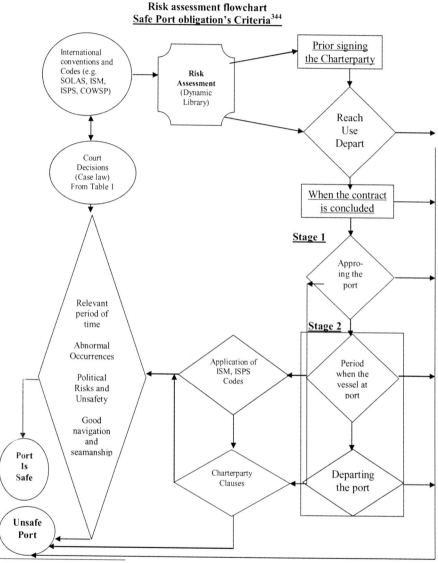

[344] E. Katarelos & A. Alexopoulos ËThe MasterÑ Role in Relation to the Safety of the Port, particularly under the concept of the ISM and the ISPS codesŜ, p.10 cited in: *www.martrans.org:8093/symposium/papers/Track%20B/B23%20katarelos%20et%20al.pdf*

Chapter Six
Conclusion

Conclusion

It is the duty of time or voyage charterers to send the ship to a safe port.[345] The obligation of safety to nominate a safe port is on both the port or berth charter.[346] Disputes concerning a safe port obligation will be treated judicially in light of Sellers\`efinition in *The Eastern City*[347]. Such definition contains the practical elements that render the port to be safe. The definition designated some duties on the charterer over the period from the moment that the charterer gives the order that the port was prospectively safe for the vessel to get into, stay as long as necessary, and safely leave.[348] The obligation of port safety will not be fulfilled unless the particular ship can reach it in the relevant period of time, use it and return from it without, in the absence of some abnormal occurrence, being exposed to danger which cannot be avoided by good navigation and seamanship.[349] There are many reasons for the ports to be unsafe such as meteorological characteristics,[350] political[351] or physical unsafety in the port layout, [352] including the size of the vessel.[353] Because of her size, she may require a tug to enter the port; the unavailability of a tug will render the port unsafe. Again, if the port requires the master to have a level of skill more than the reasonable degree expected, the port, therefore, is not unsafe.[354] Speaking of port danger, a port will not be dangerous unless the unsafety is a normal characteristic of the port.[355] But it is essential to remember that a temporary danger, i.e. a neap

---

[345] J. Wilson, Carriage of Goods by Sea, (2004, Pearson Longman), p.25
[346] Unitramp v Garnac Grain Co Inc (The Hermine) [1979] 1 Lloyd's Rep 212 (CA), 214
[347] *The Eastern City* [1958] 2 Lloyd's Rep 127
[348] *The Evia* [1982] 1 Lloyd's Rep. 334
[349] *The Eastern City* [1958] 2 Lloyd's Rep 127, p131
[350] *The Eastern City* [1958] 2 Lloyd's Rep 127
[351] *Vardinoyannis v. The Egyptian General Petroleum Corporation (The Evaggelos Th)* [1971] 2 Lloyd's Rep. 200; Ogden v Graham (1861) 1 B&S 773.
[352] *Reardon Smith Line v. Australian Wheat Board (The Houseton City)* [1956] 1 Lloyd's Rep. 1 cited in M. Wilford, T. Coghlin & J.D. Kimball, Time Charters (2003, LLP), p.198 (see also The Carnival [1992] 1 Lloyd's Rep. 449, [1994] 2 Lloyd's Rep. 14 (C.A.) where the ship was damaged by a defective fender).
[353] *Brostrom, A & Son v.Dreyfus, L & Co* [1932] 44 Ll L Rep 136
[354] *Kristiandsands Tankeri v. Standard (Bahamas) (The Polyglory)* [1977] 2 Lloyd's Rep.353.
[355] *Transoceanic Petroleum Carriers v Cook Industries Inc (The Mary Lou)* [1981] 2 Lloyd's Rep 272

tide will not render the port unsafe. [356] But a dangerous operative for a long period which may frustrate the commercial object will make the nominated port unsafe.

In terms of renomination, a time charterer has a duty to renominate a safe port if the ship, while at port, has faced a danger which still can be avoided.[357] Renomination of a safe port is different in voyage charter than in time charter. Simply, the most important reason is because the time charterer has the control of employment of the ship.[358] Whereas the voyage charterer usually fixes the destination from the beginning of the signing of the contract and he does not have that extension of the commercial control on the vessel in this matter.[359]

Although the nomination seems lawful, the master and the shipowner are not obliged to obey the charterer immediately.[360] The master can decline such nomination upon discovering the unsafety of the port and he is allowed by law to request for a fresh lawful order.[361]

The promise of safety is usually expressed in the contract, but if the nomination in the contract is silent as to its safety, the law may imply the obligation of safety.[362] However, the term will not be implied if the nomination is made to a named port e.g. to Liverpool. The shipowner has assumed the responsibility that the ship can trade there.[363]

---

[356] S. Boyd, A. Burrows & D. Foxton, (Eds.) Scrutton on Charterparties and Bill of Lading, (1996, Sweet & Maxwell), p.131.
[357] J.Cooke, T. Young, A. Taylor, J. Kimball, D. Martowski and L. Lambert, Voyage Charters, (2001, London, LLP), at 5.56.
[358] The Evia [1983] 1 AC 736 at p. 757. (HL) at p.763, Cited in C. Sun, ENomination of Ports by the Voyage ChartererŠ (1993) 5 SACLJ 207, at 212
[359] The Evia [1983] 1 AC 736 at p. 757. (HL) at p.763, Cited in C. Sun, ENomination of Ports by the Voyage ChartererŠ (1993) 5 SACLJ 207, at 212
[360] Kuwait Petroleum Corp v. I & D Oil Carriers Ltd (The Houda) [1994] 2 LloydŇ Rep. 541.
[361] Motor Oil Hellas (Corinth) Refineries v. Shipping Corp. of India (The Kanchenjunga) [1990] 1 LloydŇ Rep. 391
[362] The Aegean Sea [1998] 2 LloydŇ Rep 39.
[363] See Reardon Smith Line Ltd. V. Austalian Wheat Board (The Houston City) [1954] 2 LloydŇ Rep. 148 and Atkins International v. Islamic Republic of Iran Shipping Lines (The A.P.J. Priti) [1987] 2 LloydŇ Rep. 37. cited in J. Cooke, T. Young, A. Taylor, J. Kimball, D. Martowski & L. Lambert, Voyage Charters (2007, Informa), p. 112

In some charters, the strict obligation can be replaced by the duty to exercise due diligence as to render the charterer liable should he not exercise due diligence in nominating the port.[364] The intention of other clauses such as Ìso near thereto as she may safely getŠ believed to reduce the safety obligation by sending the ship to an alternative port, since the charterer is prevented from entering the nominated port and exposed to unreasonable delay.[365] In certain cases such as Clause 21(A) of the Baltime form, clauses have been relied upon by owners either as an alternative to, or to reinforce, a claim against the breach of the obligation of a safe port.[366] Also, the Èemployment and indemnityŠ clause is used as another way of presenting a claim for damage at an unsafe port.

The cause damage resulting from unsafe port nomination is to be indemnified by the charterer even if he was not aware of the unsafety of the port. The obligation is displaced at the occurrence of the intervening negligent act by the master should the unsafety of the port be obvious.[367] On the other hand, if the danger was not obvious, the masterÑ circumstance may be placed on the ÕhornÑ of dilemmaÑ whether he chose to proceed into the port or deny and request for a fresh order. However, if the decision was made to proceed, his act will not count as a *novus actus interveniens*[368] Yet English courts are reluctant to invoke the 1945 Act for the named contractual safe port obligation. Though, the defendantÑ liability was the same both in tort of negligence and in contract, the 1945 Act may apply.[369]

Since the ISM code primary aim is to establish an international standard for safe management and operation of ships, the extent of such standard covers the safety of the ports and their potential hazards on the vessels. The principle of ISPS is believed[370] to be the same. ISPS code

---

[364] *The Chemical Venture* [1993] 1 LloydÑ Rep. 508.
[365] *Dahl* v. *Velson* (1880) 6 App. Cas.38 cited in Voyage charters. P.131
[366] H. Baker & P. David, ÈThe politically unsafe portŠ, LMCL, p.112 at p.127.
[367] *Compania Naviera Maropan S.S. v. Bowaters Lloyd Pulp and Paper Mills Ltd. (The Stork)*[1955] 2 Q.B. 68, Per Singleton J. at p.89 the same point was raised in the judgement of Delvin J. in the same case at p. 77.
[368] *The Stork* (1955) 2 QB 68.
[369] *Forsikringsaktieselskapet Vesta v. Butcher* [1986] 2 All E.R. 488, noted by L.J. Anderson [1987] 1 LMCLQ 10.
[370] P. Anderson, ÈSession 5-ISM and ISPS Codes-influence on the Evolution LiabilityŠ, International Colloquium on Maritime Legal Liabilities, 14-15 Sept. 2006 at The Institute of International Shipping and Trade Law, University of Wales, Swansea.

lays down procedures for adoption by port managers and shipowners to safeguard the future of shipping and ports from terrorist attacks.[371] The author is of the opinion that ISM, ISPS and case law could possibly be used as a tool of risk assessment. The master may carry out a risk assessment model in order to lead him to two clear assumptions: whether the port is a safe port or an unsafe port. Consequently, should the disputes allegedly arise due to the unsafety of the port, the court may adopt the risk assessment model to clear the doubt of whether the master is negligent in his discretion whether to enter the port or not. Finally, the author is also of the opinion that the model of risk assessment, if it is not used by the master, may consist of negligence in the duty of the shipowner. In contrast, if the suggested model is invoked, it may well be a great help for the court to replace the dicta on the part of the master when he is placed on the ďhorn of dilemmaÑ

---

[371] B. Soyer & R. Williams, ĐPotential Legal Ramifications of the International Ship and Port Facility Security (ISPS) Code on Maritime LawŠ, 2005 LMCLQ. p.515.

Glossary

Anchor dragging is when an anchor for any reason is not holding its position e.g. bad holding on the seabed, or high weight in the anchor.

Bar. (A bar draught) is a sandbank which forms at the mouths of rivers and very often limits the type of ship able to reach up-river destinations. In many cases, ships have to lighten, that is, to discharge some of their cargo to barges or small ships, before being able to navigate over a bar and complete the voyage. Equally, ships loading at an up-river port may only be able to load part of the cargo, the balance being taken on board after the ship has cleared the bar.

COSWP. (Code of Safe Working Practice) contains 33 chapters. Chapter 1 concern the risk assessment. An industrial code of practice is a simple and flexible extension of the law. It generally specifies technical and other legal requirements in more detail or in liberal style than is practical or desirable in regulations. Failure to observe any provision of a code of practice will not in itself render a person liable to criminal or civil proceeding; a person cannot be prosecuted for breaching a provision of a code of practice. It can be used as evidence of failure to observe the codeÑ provision will generally be proof of contravention of the statutory provision. The COSWP gives advice on the roles of those with particular safety responsibilities, and highlight work areas where specific responsibilities should be allocated.

Berth: place in a port alongside a quay where a ship loads or discharge cargo or, in the case of lay-by berth, waits until a loading or discharging berth is available. This term is also frequently used to signify a place alongside a quay, each of which is capable of accommodating only one ship at a time.

Dolphin. A mooring buoy or spar used for mooring.

Fender. Rubber, Wood or Rope used over the side to protect a vessel from chafing when alongside a jetty or berth.

Hauling off buoy. A buoy used to keep the ship in position by hauling the slack of the shipÑ mooring rope.

IMO. The International Maritime Organization (until 1982 the Inter-governmental Maritime Consultative Organization) is a special agency of the United Nations that has been responsible for the preparation and implementation of many important international conventions on maritime conventions such as the 1974 Safety of Life at Sea Convention (SOLAS).

ISM. The International Safety Management Code. The Code made mandatory by means of a reference in Chapter IX of (SOLAS). Companies which companies with the ISM Code should be issued with Document of Compliance, a copy of which should be kept on board. Administrations should also issue a safety management certificate to indicate that the company operates in accordance with the safety management system (SMS) and periodic checks should be carried out to verify that the ship̃ SMS is functioning properly.

ISPS. Contain detailed security-related requirements for governments, port authorities and shipping companies in a mandatory section (Part A), together with guidelines on how to meet these requirements in a non-mandatory section (Part B). Essentially requires security to be treated as a risk management problem. Requirements for ship include Ship Security Plans, Ship Security Officers, Company Security Officers, and certain on-board equipment. Applies to all passenger ships and cargo ships. Adopted December 2002 under new SOLAS chapter XI-2 (special measures to enhance maritime security). In force 1 July 2004.

Mooring buoy. A buoy secured to a permanent anchor sunk deeply into the bottom used to moor the ship in position.

Navigational aids include any object that a navigator (ship̃ master) may use to find his position, such as permanent land or sea markers, buoys, radio beacons and lighthouses.

Neap tide. Is a tide whose range between high and low water is at its lowest. Neap tide occurs shortly after first and third quarter. A ship which is unable to leave a port or place because a neap tide is said to be neaped.

Risk assessment. Is a process that evaluates how likely is that a set of hazardous circumstances will arise and estimate the potential consequences in order to avoid it.

Seamanship. All the arts and skills of ship handling, ranging from maintenance and repairs. It is the required proper practical experience required by the seamen in carrying his duty.

Unmarked wreck An unidentified submerged wreck which is hazard to navigation. an example of unmarked wreck where a shoal that is not indicated by the means of navigational buoys.

Yaw. When the whole ship moves bodily to port and then to starboard around it vertical axis. It is one of the 6 bodily motions of the ship.

Bibliography

Anderson, P. ISM Code: a practical guide to the legal and insurance implications (2005, LLP, 2nd edn.)

Anderson, P. Paper on ÈSM and ISPS Codes-Influence on the Evolution of LiabilitiesŠ, International Colloquium on Maritime Legal Liabilities (14-15 September 2006) in The Institute of International Shipping and Trade Law, University of Wales, Swansea

Anderson, P. ÈThe Errors of Our Ways!Š (2007) MRI, Vol. 21(2), pp.16-17

Astle, W.E. International Cargo Carriers liability (1984, Fairplay Publications)

Astle, W.E. The Safe Port (1986, Fairplay Publications)

Baker, C. ÈThe safe port/berth obligation and employment and indemnity clausesŠ (1988) LMCLQ, p.43

Baker, H. & David, P. ÈThe politically unsafe portŠ (1986) LMCLQ, p.112

Baughen, S. Shipping Law (2004, Cavendish Publishing)

Bennett, H. ÈSafe Port ClausesŠ, cited as Chapter 4 in D.R. Thomas, Legal Issues Relating to Time Charterparties (2008, Informa)

Billington, ÈManaging Risk in PortsŠ as Chapter 4 in C.J. Parker. Managing Risk in Shipping (1999, Nautical Institute)

Boyd, S., Burrows, A. & Foxton, D. (eds.) Scrutton on Charterparties and Bill of Lading, (1996, Sweet & Maxwell)

Carr, I. International Trade Law, (2005, Cavendish Publishing)

Chan, L.S. ÈNomination of Ports by the Voyage ChartererŠ (1993) Vol.5, SACLJ,   p. 207

Chong, D.G.S ÈRevisiting the Safe PortŠ (1992) SJLS p.79

Chuah, J. Law of International Trade (2005, Sweet & Maxwell)

Cooke, J., Young, T., Taylor, A., Kimball, J., Martowski, D. & Lambert, L. Voyage Charters (2007 3rd edn., Informa)

Davenport, B.J. ÈUnsafe Ports Again: The Sage CobŠ (1993) LMCLQ, p.150.

Davies, M. & Dickey, A. Shipping Law (2004, LLP)

Dockray, M. Cases and materials on the Carriage of Goods by Sea (2004, Cavendish Publishing)

ExpertÑ advice and consultancy listed in Specialist firm on ISM and risk assessment (consultISM) site, on: www.Consultism.co.uk/client.html.charterers

Gardner, D. ÈTerrorist Attacks - Being PreparedŠ (December, 2005) cited as electronic article in Curtis Davis Garrard law firm site: http://www.cdg.co.uk/articles_ view.php?pid=12&action=VIEW&news_id=88&type_id=4.

Gaskell, N.J., Debattista, C. & Swatton, R.J. Chorley & GilesÑShipping Law (2001, Pitman Publishing)

Girvin, S. Carriage of Goods by Sea (2007, Oxford University Press)

Gold, E., Chircop, A. & Kindred, H.M. Maritime Law (2003, Canada: Irwin Law)

Gorton, L., Ihre, R., Sandevärn, A. & Hillenius, P. Shipbroking and Chartering Practice, (1999, LLP)

Grime, R. Shipping Law, (1991, 2nd edn, Sweet & Maxwell),

Hartman, P. ÈSafe Port/Berth Clauses: Warranty or Due Diligence?Š Vol.21, TML J p.540 (1996-1997)

Hill, C. Maritime Law (1998, LLP)

Holden, J.M. PaynesÑ Carriage of Goods by Sea, (1954, Butterworth)

Hughes, A.D. Casebook on Carriage of Goods by Sea (Blackstone Press Ltd, 1999)

Ivamy, H. Payne & IvamyÑ Carriage of Good by Sea, (1989, Butterworth)

Katarelos, E. & Alexopoulos, A. ÈThe MasterÑ Role in Relation to the Safety of the Port, particularly under the Concept of the ISM and the ISPS CodesŠ, electronic articles cited in www.martrans.org:8093/symposium/papers/ Track%20B/ B23% 20katarelos%20et%20al.pdf

Maclachlan, M. The Shipmaster'ŝ Business Companion (2004, Nautical Institute)

Mandaraka-Sheppard, A. Modern Maritime Law and Risk Management (2007, Cavendish Publishing)

Mankabady, S. ÈThe Concept of Safe PortŠ (1973-1974) 5 JML&C 633

Michel, K. War, Terror and Carriage by Sea (2004, LLP)

Miller, M.D. Marine War Risks (1994, LLP)

Oil Companies International Marine Forum, Tanker management and self assessment: A best-practice guide for ship operators (2004, Witherby & Co. Ltd, 1st edn.)

Schroder, T. ÈUnsafe ports on account of iceŠ The Swedish Club letter 2 (2006)

Soyer, P. & Williams, R. ÈPotential Legal Ramifications of the International Ship and Port Facility Security (ISPS) Code on Maritime LawŠ (2005) LMCLQ, p.515

Wilford, M., Coghlin, T. & Kimball, J.D. Time Charters (2003, LLP)

Williams, H. Chartering Documents (1999, LLP)

Wilson, J. Carriage of Goods by Sea, (1998, Pitman Publishing)

Yates, D. Contracts for the Carriage of Goods by Land, Sea and Air (1993, LLP)

Printed by
Schaltungsdienst Lange o.H.G., Berlin